The Sacred Path

OTHER BOOKS EDITED BY
JOHN BIERHORST

The Sacred Path

SPELLS, PRAYERS & POWER SONGS

OF THE AMERICAN INDIANS

Edited by John Bierhorst

WILLIAM MORROW AND COMPANY

New York 1983

1   2   3   4   5   6   7   8   9   10

Library of Congress Cataloging in Publication Data
Main entry under title:

The Sacred path.

Includes bibliographical references.
Summary: English translations of North and
South American Indian spells, prayers, and songs
traditionally used in rituals associated with
birth, puberty, love, travel, sickness,
weather, farming, hunting, and death.
1. Indian poetry—Translations into English.
2. American poetry—Translations from Indian languages.
3. Indians—Religion and mythology.   4. Indians—Magic.
[1. Indian poetry—Collections.   2. Indians—Religion
and mythology.   3. Indians—Magic]   I. Bierhorst, John.
PM197.E3S22   1983   897   82-14118
ISBN 0-688-01699-5

Frontispiece / Pair of Navajo
prayer sticks, each with a
jeweled string representing the
path of life (*Memoirs of the Amer.
Mus. of Nat. Hist., vol. 6*).

Acknowledgment is made to the copyright holders for permission to reprint from the following (for titles of the selections reprinted, see Notes): Boas, Franz, *Kwakiutl Ethnography,* © 1966 by The University of Chicago (by permission of The University of Chicago Press); Carpenter, Edmund, *Anerca,* J. M. Dent and Sons, 1959 (by permission of the author); Curtis, Natalie, *The Indians' Book,* Dover Publications, 1968; Estrada, Alvaro, *María Sabina: Her Life and Chants,* translated from the Spanish by Henry Munn, preface by Jerome Rothenberg, retrospective essay by R. Gordon Wasson, Ross-Erikson, Inc., 1981; Hart-González, Lucinda, et al., *Latin American Indian Literatures,* Northwestern Pennsylvania Institute for Latin American Studies and Mercyhurst College, Erie, Pa., 1980; Kilpatrick, Jack F. and Anna G., *Run Toward the Nightland,* © 1967, Southern Methodist University Press, and *Walk in Your Soul,* © 1965, Southern Methodist University Press; Luckert, Karl W., *Coyoteway: A Navajo Holyway Healing Ceremonial,* University of Arizona Press and Museum of Northern Arizona Press, 1979; Merriam, Alan P., "Songs and Dances of the Flathead Indians," Folkways Records, 1953; Ortiz, Alfonso, *The Tewa World: Space, Time, Being, and Becoming in a Pueblo Society,* © 1969 by The University of Chicago (by permission of The University of Chicago Press); Ray, Verne F., *Primitive Pragmatists: The Modoc Indians of Northern California,* University of Washington Press, 1963; Reichard, Gladys, *Prayer: The Compulsive Word,* University of Washington Press, 1944; Underhill, Ruth M., *Papago Indian Religion,* Columbia University Press, 1946; Underhill, Ruth M., Bahr, Donald M., Lopez, B., Pancho, J., and Lopez, D., *Rainhouse and Ocean: Speeches for the Papago Year,* American Tribal Religions, vol. 4, Museum of Northern Arizona, 1979, distributed by University of Nebraska Press (by permission of Karl W. Luckert); Weltfish, Gene, "Music of the Pawnee," Folkways Records, 1965; Wyman, Leland C., *Blessingway,* University of Arizona Press, 1970.

Acknowledgment is made to the copyright holders for permission to translate from the following (for titles of selections translated, see Notes); Preuss, Konrad Theodor, *Religion und Mythologie der Uitoto,* Vandenhoeck & Ruprecht, 1921–23; Victor, Paul-Emile, *Poèmes esquimaux,* 2d ed., Pierre Seghers, 1951 (by permission of Editions Robert Laffont, Paris).

Contents

AGAINST SICKNESS AND EVIL

CONTROLLING THE WEATHER

PLANTING AND GATHERING

FOR THE HUNTER

FOR THE DYING AND THE DEAD

The Sacred Path

INTRODUCTION

I

The belief that words in themselves have the power to make things happen—especially words in extraordinary combinations—is one of the distinguishing features of native American thought; and it may be said that for the people who share this belief a connection exists between the sacred and the verbal, or, to put it in more familiar terms, a connection between religion and poetry.

When the connection is broken, poetry begins to lose its audience. It may still be admired, but it comes to be recognized as a form of self-expression, unable to establish contact with supernatural forces. Not surprisingly, the word "poetry," as it is understood in English today, has no precise equivalent in native American languages. What are thought of by outsiders as Indian "poems" are actually spells, prayers, or words to songs. Though often appreciated as beautiful, they are seldom recited purely for entertainment. Rather, they are used for gaining control or for making things turn out right. Poetry of this sort, so long as the culture that produced it remains intact, is not in danger of losing its audience.

Indian prayers and songs, at least formerly, were used in times of crisis and in connection with every major undertaking. The ability to recite them was equated with wisdom, and in certain Indian communities they were regarded as a form of wealth; to have had none was to be poor. Even today they have not completely lost their original importance, especially in the southwestern United States, in parts of Mexico, and in tropical South America. For the outsider, their value lies in their vivid, highly condensed portrayal of Indian customs, on the one hand, and, on the other, their authoritative language, which even in translation has the ability to exert an influence on the mind, if not on the physical world.

3

Songs and prayers are used in connection with the three predictable crises in the life of the individual: birth, puberty, and death. In childbirth, the primary concern is for the safety of the mother. For her sake it is hoped that the birth will be quick and painless. After the child has been delivered, prayers are necessary to protect the child and to make it strong. At puberty, special words prepare the boy for manhood and the girl for womanhood. At death, prayers help to separate the survivors from the deceased and to speed the ghost on its way to the next world.

Rituals of initiation into secret societies, often medicine societies, may occur at puberty. But they may also occur in adulthood, even in middle age, providing the older person with an opportunity to renew his life. Sickness itself is a time of change and is typically accompanied by magic spells, prayers, or medicine songs. These often derive from dreams or hallucinations and are among the most imaginative specimens of American Indian poetry.

Though important socially, marriage holds little religious significance and gives rise to virtually no poetry. An anthology of American Indian wedding songs would be all but impossible to compile for lack of material. However, love spells and love songs are well developed in many tribes, and in puberty ceremonies one of the recurring themes is preparation for marriage.

Prayers are needed to control the weather, to ensure success in hunting, and to promote the growth of crops. In many cases, especially where planting and harvesting are concerned, these rituals become large-scale public ceremonies involving the entire community.

3

The differences between spells, prayers, and songs may be blurred if spells or prayers are sung or if spells are softened to include the beseeching, wishful phrases typical of prayers. In general, the spell is a set of directions, the prayer is a request, and the song is a description. Each in its own way is calculated to bring about a desired result.

Non-Indians are quick to recognize spells as a form of magic. These have an insistent, compulsive quality associated with witchcraft and are often referred to as charms, formulas, or incantations. Some indeed are used for dark purposes; for example, to destroy an enemy. But by far the greatest number are designed to cure sickness. Many cradlesongs and lullabies are gentle spells, crooned softly in order to put a baby to sleep.

Sir Edward B. Tylor's often-quoted definition of prayer ("the address of personal spirit to personal spirit") applies particularly well to the supplications used by the Indians of the Plains. These ritual addresses to the power known variously as Wakonda, Father, You Above, or He That Hears Always are likely to strike the modern American mind as all that prayer should be: heartfelt, imploring, promissory, and with signs of contrition. In fact, the weeping and self-mortification that sometimes accompany such prayers are calculated to arouse supernatural pity; and often the supplicant expects—and receives—an apparition. Yet the forceful, insistent language of spells is virtually unknown to the Sioux, Arapaho, Crow, and other Plains tribes. In the Southwest, however, especially among the Navajo and the Zuni, so-called prayers tend to be equal mixtures of prayer and spell.

The naked spell can seldom if ever be used in the presence of a large gathering. It must be weakened to accommodate the socially acceptable "please" or "maybe" of the prayer or shifted to the purely descriptive realm of the song.

The Indian songs most admired by outsiders have brief, impressionistic texts reminiscent of Japanese *haiku*. For example: "A bubbling spring comes from the hard ground," or "I, the song, I walk here" (the first is from the Chippewa, the second from the Modoc). But these are really power songs, each of whose miniature texts condenses an important idea connected with healing.

If I say "May you live long," the meaning is plain enough. But if I change it to read "May you live until your hair is white," substituting white hair for old age, the words qualify as poetry. If I say "May you fall asleep old," substituting sleep for death, the basic meaning is still there ("May you live long"), but the expression is tinged with a certain mystery. I am wishing you well, while in fact my words refer to your death. We may say that the poetry has here been raised to a new level.

Substitutions of this sort, whether simple or complex, are well known to American Indian ritualists. Among the Papago they are called "soft words," words whose meaning is somewhat hidden. "Soft words" must be used in the presence of supernatual power, where to speak openly might be dangerous. Among the Aztecs such word substitutions, or metaphors, were called *machiyotlatolli,* meaning "comparative speech," and were considered appropriate for songs, prayers, and elegant oratory.

Among the most widespread metaphors in Indian poetry are those in which good health is compared to sunrise, or the lifetime of the individual is compared to a path, or road. When the Zuni ritualist says, "May your road reach to Dawn Lake" he means, "May you live long." When the Sioux prayer maker speaks of walking the "sacred path," he refers to the journey through life, which he hopes will be blessed by the gods.

In the Eskimo love poem on page 47, an extended comparison likens the loved one to the seal as it is pursued by the hunter. The idea of comparing the thing one loves to the thing one wishes to kill is more than a mere figure of speech. It is mysterious. The connection between love and death is made again in the Quechua song entitled "Keeping a Fly" (page 56).

In the Navajo prayer to the dead buck (page 136) the hunter imagines that the animal he has killed has just been reborn. The substitution of birth for death, like the substitution of death for love, is typical of myth, ritual, and primitive poetry in general. It creates mystery in the religious sense. In other words, the connection is deeply felt, though we may be unable to explain exactly why it exists.

5

It will be noticed that this book includes illustrations of American Indian fetishes and prayer sticks. These are aids to make prayer more effective or, in some cases, substitutes for prayer itself.

A fetish is an object such as a stone, a skull, a feather, or a doll that is believed to increase the supernatural power of the person who uses it. Often a spirit is thought to live inside the object, as with Zuni hunting fetishes, which are said to be the shrunken images of the great animal gods that control both hunting and war. The hunter or warrior prays directly to the fetish and either breathes *on* it or breathes *from* it.

In many cases, masks may be regarded as fetishes. When worn by the dancer, the mask converts the wearer into a god. Detached from the dancer, it becomes an object of sacred power, which may be prayed to. Sometimes bits of food are given to it as a sacrificial offering.

Prayer sticks are symbolic prayers typical of the Indians of the Southwest, who believe that the stick with its special decorations conveys a message to the spirits. Sometimes it is merely thought of as an offering, but often it actually stands for words or sentences. The Navajo prayer sticks shown opposite the title page of this book, with their cotton strings symbolizing the path of life, include feathers of the turkey (a bird of the earth) and of the eagle (a bird of the sky), representing the words "with beauty below me may I walk" and "with beauty above me may I walk." The strings pass through jewels, symbolizing the words "with beauty all around me may I walk."

The Huichol, who live in northwestern Mexico, make their

prayer sticks from arrows, believing that the prayers are "shot" to the gods, just as an arrow is shot from a bow. A prayer arrow used by a woman is shown on page 44.

A great many prayer sticks and fetishes are either made of or are decorated with feathers, and it is interesting to observe how often the feathers are put together in pairs. For the most part, the reasons are unrecorded. However, a common idea is that feathers, like the birds from which they are taken, have the ability to rise upward, perhaps making contact with the sky world. The burning of incense in connection with the recitation of prayers expresses a similar belief: the smoke rises into the sky, reaching the spirits who live there.

6

In an earlier anthology of Indian poetry, entitled *In the Trail of the Wind,* I tried to give a sense of native American history, beginning with mythic times and continuing into the twentieth century. By contrast, the present collection focuses on the life of the individual, emphasizing the connection between ritual poetry and personal needs. The thematic groupings are an attempt to make this connection clear, and in a few cases procedural details are given in order to show how the texts are actually used. These instructions are printed in italics, enclosed in diagonal slashes. For example, / *The warrior opens his pouch . . .* / in the prayer on page 70, or / *He whistles* / in the chant on page 89. If the instructions are given in the words of the native informant, slashes are not used, as on pages 36 and 129. It should be kept in mind that Indian prayers and spells, and to a lesser extent songs, are performances in which the action may be as important as the text.

So far as it is possible to do so, the selections have been arranged in an orderly sequence, not only to ease the transition from one page to the next but to minimize the need for explanatory notes.

For example, the Cherokee spell for putting a woman's family to sleep (page 54) is immediately followed by the famous Inca song in which the lover imagines himself stealing into the woman's bedroom. When read in sequence, the two selections help to explain each other.

The difficult Papago prayer about "putting" things on the body of the dead deer (page 135) is clarified, one hopes, by a reading of the Navajo prayer to the dead buck (page 136). In this case, since the Papago and the Navajo are near neighbors, the similarity may be more than coincidental.

Particular care has been taken to choose translations that accurately reflect the native texts. In a few places it has been possible to correct older versions in the light of recent scholarship. Wherever this is done, mention is made in the notes. Possible errors and inconsistencies have been allowed to stand, however, if there is room for doubt. Thus the Navajo spirit *Anilthani* appears as "grasshopper" in Washington Matthews' translation of 1887 (see page 105) and as "Cornbeetle" in Leland Wyman's translation of 1970 (see page 13).

The older sources of Indian prayers, spells, and songs, especially those dating from the period 1880–1920, while still important, are no longer as essential as they once were. It will be found that a large share of the selections in this book date from 1920–70; and fully a third either draw upon sources that have become available since 1970 or, if taken from older sources, have been newly translated. It is hoped, therefore, that this volume will hold a measure of interest for the growing number of readers already attuned to traditional Indian poetry, while serving as an invitation to those who are as yet unacquainted.

J.B.

Birth and Infancy

Huichol fetish representing
Grandmother Growth, who
prays for the health of children
(*Memoirs of the Amer. Mus. of
Nat. Hist., vol. 3*).

Mother's Prayer for a Girl

May I give birth to Pollen Girl, may I give birth to Cornbee-
    tle Girl, may I give birth to Long-Life Girl, may I give
    birth to Happiness Girl.
With long-life-happiness surrounding me may I in blessing
    give birth. May I quickly give birth.
In blessing may I arise again, in blessing may I recover. As
    one who is long-life-happiness may I live on.

NAVAJO

Magic Spell for a Difficult Birth

Daughter of the great earth,
good young woman with legs opened to give birth,
good young woman cursed by evil ones,
I take out the child,
I make it come out.
I do it for her,
whose descendants will call her name,
and she will be their power.
I make her give birth,
I make her strong.

AREKUNA

Song to the Child

That she was taken out of her mother, thanks be for that!
That she, the little one, was taken out of her, we say, thanks
    be for that!

WEST GREENLAND ESKIMO

Song to a Son

O great one, source of surprise!
O great one, master!
Welcome, master!
Welcome! You will be a fisherman, master!

KWAKIUTL

Prayer of a Man to Twin Children

O Supernatural Ones, you have come, you have arrived and
    you have come to be supernatural for us; you who come
    from the sea, Rich-Makers, Swimmers.
Now, thank you for coming to us, to me and to your mother,
    that she may come and treat you well and you also treat
    us well.
Do not let anything evil befall us, you, Long-Life-Makers,
    only protect us, Supernatural Ones.

KWAKIUTL

Prayer of the Midwife to the
Goddess of Water

Noble One, Our Great One, Skirt of Jade, Jade-that-shines,
    a child has arrived,

Sent by our mother, our father, Two Lord, Two Lady, from
    above the nine heavens, from Where-There-Are-Two.

But endowed with what? Given what in the ancient night?
    How fated, how wrapped, how clothed?

Ah, perhaps he has not been born in peace. Ah, what good,
    or evil, of the mother and father comes with him?

What stain, what filth, what vileness of the mother and fa-
    ther comes with this child?

Because of this he is in your hands. Receive him, bathe him,
    wash him. For you are the one. You know the way. In-
    deed, he is left in your hands. Remove the stain, the
    filth, the vileness of the mother and father.

Perhaps he has not come in peace. May whatever comes with
    him be washed away. Let it disappear.

May his heart, his life, become good, perfect, and pure, so
    that he may live beautifully, calmly on earth.

Let it be washed out: the sin, the corruption. Let it be
    washed out, let it disappear, flowing away.

He is in your hands, O Noble One, Our Great One, Jade
    Woman, Jade skirt, Jade-that-shines, mother of gods,
    sister of gods. The child has been left in your hands.

For this is your lot and your portion: this you were granted in the ancient night: that you wash, that you clean this child who has come before you. May your heart be generous, Our Great One!

AZTEC

Introduction to Life

/ As the mother holds the baby in her arms, the shaman, with his lips close to the child's face, utters these words: /

I arise from rest with movements swift
As the beat of a raven's wings
I arise
To meet the day
Wa—wa.
My face is turned from the dark of night
To gaze at the dawn of day
Now whitening in the sky.

IGLULIK ESKIMO

Woman's Prayer to the Sun,
for a Newborn Girl

Your beautiful rays,
may they color our faces;
being dyed in them,
somewhere at an old age
we shall fall asleep old women.

HOPI

When the Child Is Named

*/ The mother and the godmother stand on the housetop before dawn; the god-
mother speaks: /*

My sun!
My morning star!
Help this child to become a man.
I name him
Rain-dew Falling!
I name him
Star Mountain!

/ The mother throws a live coal; the godmother throws sacred meal. /

TEWA

Lullaby

Baby swimming down the river:
Little driftwood legs,
Little rabbit legs.

KIOWA

Cradlesong

Sleep, little one, your father is bringing
a spotted deer to be your pet,
a rabbit's ear to be your necklace,
spotted bramble fruits to be your toys.

MBYÁ

Cradlesong for Ahuitzotl

Little jewel, stop crying,
you little babe, I'll lay you
in your cradle, little Ahuitzotl,
your father will come, he will rock you,
iyao ohuiya.

My heart enjoys it,
I've made you,
my little babe, little Ahuitzotl,
your father will come, he will rock you,
iyao ohuiya.

AZTEC

Lullaby

Baby, sleep, sleep, sleep
Father has gone to find turtle shells
He said he will come back tomorrow
Baby, sleep, sleep, sleep

CREEK

Words to a Sick Child

Little child! Your mother's breasts are full of milk.
Go and be nursed,
Go and drink!
Go up to the mountain!
From the summit of the mountain you shall seek health,
You shall draw life.

IGLULIK ESKIMO

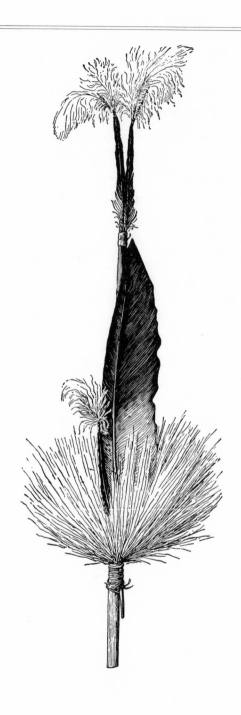

Growing Up

Eskimo dance wand, carried by
women (*18th An. Rep. of the Bur.
of Amer. Ethnology*).

Prayer of the Youngest Daughter, with an Offering of Crumbs

Grandfathers, here, eat! May I become a woman, and may
    my older brothers and older sisters reach young man-
    hood and young womanhood!

ZUNI

Prayer of an Old Man at a Young Man's Change of Name

My grandfather, the sun, you who walk yellow, look down
  on us. Pity us. Pity us. May this young man facing
  straight be helped to walk for his life!
Those that shine above at night, and the animals of the
  night, we pray to you.
The morning star and my father, listen. I have asked for long
  breath, for large life.
May this young man, with his people and his relatives, do
  well, walking where it is good, obtaining food and
  clothing and horses of many colors, and where there are
  birds that are crying and the day is long and the wind is
  good!
Animals that move on the surface, animals under ground
  that inhabit the water, listen, be attentive. This one
  standing here asks of you a name that is good.

ARAPAHO

Prayer

Father, Great Spirit, behold this boy! Your ways he shall see!

SIOUX

Young Man's Prayer to the Spirits

He That Hears Always, hear my cries. As my tears drop to
  the ground, look upon me.

/ *The young man grovels on the earth, tearing up grass and weeds. Then he
hacks off a fingertip, or very often he cuts around the second joint, puts the
finger between his teeth, and tears it off; then, holding the severed portion to
the sky, he cries:* /

Spirits! I give you this, my body.

May I have many horses, and many women of good looks
  and industry in my lodge.

May my lodge be the gathering place of men.

I am poor; give me these things that through me my people
  may be bold because I live.

Let them use me as a shield against the enemy!

CROW

For Young Men Growing Up,
to Help Themselves

Now! I am as beautiful as the very blossoms themselves!

I am a man, you lovely ones, you women of the Seven Clans!
Now these are my people, _____, and this is my name, _____.

Now! You women who reside among the Seven Peoples, I
have just come to intrude myself among you.

All of you have just come to gaze upon me alone, the most
beautiful.

Now! You lovely women, already I just took your souls!

I am a man!
You women will live in the very middle of my soul.

Forever I will be as beautiful as the bright red blossoms!

CHEROKEE

A Prayer of the Girls'
Puberty Ceremony

They come to the holy girl early in the morning. When she is thus holy she becomes White-Shell Woman. They also seek out a young boy and bring him there. An old man comes also. From different directions a number of old women come together who sit and pray. Sitting outside, they smoke and pray for the girl, White-Painted Woman, saying:

May you be renewed,

May I live happily.

With strewed pollen may I live happily.

This boy, too, Child of the Water, may he become new.

May I be well.

May I live to old age.

With scattered jewel dust may I live to old age.

May the pollen be on top of my feet.

JICARILLA APACHE

A Song of the Girls' Puberty Ceremony

When the earth was made;
When the sky was made;
When my songs were first heard;
The holy mountain was standing toward me with life.

At the center of the sky, the holy boy walks four ways with
    life.
Just mine, my mountain became; standing toward me with
    life.
The dancers became; standing toward me with life.
When the sun goes down to the earth, where Mescal Moun-
    tain lies with its head toward the sunrise,
Black spruce became; standing up with me.

WHITE MOUNTAIN APACHE

A Song of the Girls' Puberty Ceremony

You will be running to the four corners of the universe:
To where the land meets the big water;
To where the sky meets the land;
To where the home of winter is;
To the home of rain.
Run this! Run!
Be strong!
For you are the mother of a people.

MESCALERO APACHE

Prayer

Sun, we pray.
You know everything,
You see everything on this earth.
Make this girl healthy and strong.
Make her industrious and not lazy.
Let her have many children without pain.

PAVIOTSO

From a Prayer Summoning the Novice for His Initiation

After our moon mother,
At her sacred place,
Still small, appeared,
And now yonder in the east
Standing fully grown makes her days,
Now our spring children,
Whoever truly desires in his heart to grow old,
Taking prayer meal,
Taking shell,
Taking corn pollen,
Yonder with prayers
One by one shall make their roads go forth.

ZUNI

From a Prayer for the Novice at the Close of His Initiation

Do not despise the breath of your fathers,
But draw it into your body.
That our roads may reach to where the life-giving
      road of our sun father comes out,
That, clasping one another tight,
Holding one another fast,
We may finish our roads together;
That this may be, I add to your breath now.
To this end:
May my father bless you with life;
May your road reach to Dawn Lake,
May your road be fulfilled.

ZUNI

Initiation Songs

1

In the center
I am standing

2

In form like a bird
it appears

3

The ground trembles
as I am about to enter

4

My heart fails me
as I am about to enter
the spirit lodge

5

We are now
to receive you into the Midéwiwin
our Midé brother

6

A bubbling spring
comes from the hard ground

CHIPPEWA

Love Songs and Love Magic

Huichol prayer arrow with a
pair of miniature sandals tied
around the shaft, representing
a woman's prayer that she will
have a husband (*Memoirs of the
Amer. Mus. of Nat. Hist., vol. 3*).

The Dream

Last night I dreamed of you.
I dreamed you were walking on the shore pebbles
and I was walking with you.
Last night I dreamed of you.
And as though I were awake,
I dreamed that I followed you,
that I wanted you like a young seal,
that you were wanted by me
the way the hunter
wants a young seal
that dives when it feels it is being followed.
That's how you were wanted
by me,
who dreamed of you.

AMMASSALIK ESKIMO

Magic Spell for Finding a Woman

Mirror Land, a meeting place.
I call for a woman, sing out for a woman, crying up and
    crying down,
bringing along my helper, Xochiquetzal, dressed in a snake,
    with a snake at her hips, around her loins.
Yesterday, the day before, I wept, I cried.
But this is true spirit, true power.
Tomorrow? The next day?
Today.
It is I, the young warrior.
I shine, I dawn.
Risen from nowhere? Born from nowhere?
Risen from the flower of a woman! Born from the flower of a
    woman!
This is true spirit, true power.
Will I find her tomorrow? The next day?
Today.
It is I, the young warrior.
Am I truly a warrior? Not of war am I, but of woman.

AZTEC

Dance Song

That princess who can't love—
We'll throw her into the sweet waters of the lake.
There, there she'll learn,
Drinking those sweet waters,
That I'm to be wanted,
That I'm to be loved.

That woman who can't love—
We'll throw her into the barren snowfield.
There, there she'll learn,
Chilled by the white snow,
That I'm to be wanted,
That I'm to be loved.

That girl who can't love—
We'll drag her to the bridge, throw her into the muddy
      waters of the river.
There, there she'll learn,
Drinking those muddy waters,
That I'm to be wanted,
That I'm to be loved.

QUECHUA

Woman's Prayer

Rudá! Rudá!
O you who dwell in the skies,
Who love the rain—
O you who dwell in the skies!
Make it be that he will find all other
      women unattractive.
Let him think of me,
When the sun disappears in the west.

ANAMBÉ

Man's Song

It is my form and person that makes me great.
Hear the voice of my song—it is my voice.
I shield myself with secret coverings.
All your thoughts are known to me—blush!
I could draw you hence, were you on a distant island; though
    you were on the other hemisphere.
I speak to your naked heart.

CHIPPEWA

Magic Spell to Turn a Woman's Heart

Here,
here am I,
a poor one.
I turn this good young woman,
daughter of the ancient ones,
toward me,
toward myself,
toward my eyebrows,
toward my head,
toward my arms,
toward my chest,
toward my hands,
toward my legs,
toward my heart.
I leave nothing unnamed.

AREKUNA

To Fix the Affections

I am as Red, as beautiful as the Rainbow.

Your heart has just been taken by me.

Your blood has been taken by me.

Your flesh has been taken by me.

Your eyes have been taken by me.

Your saliva has been taken by me.

Your saliva and mine are one forever.
You are a Wizard!

CHEROKEE

For Putting a Woman's Family to Sleep

People, sleep is coming!

Very quickly all of you are turning over.

Night is coming.

Keep on throughout the night: the Dark Moon has just come
to live in your soul!

CHEROKEE

Song

In an accessible place
you will sleep.
At midnight
I will come.

INCA

Keeping a Fly

I'm keeping a fly
with wings of gold,
keeping a fly
with eyes of fire,

with death in its eyes of fire,
death
in its hairs of gold,
in its lovely wings,

keeping it
—in a ginger ale bottle.
Nobody knows if it drinks,
nobody knows if it eats.

It wanders at night
like a star,
kills with a bursting red glow
in its eyes of fire,

love in its eyes of fire,
love that it holds in its heart,
its blood,
glowing in the night.

Insect of the night,
fly, carrier of death,
in a green bottle I keep it,
loving it so.

But, of course, of course,
nobody knows
if I let it drink,
if I let it eat.

QUECHUA

Man's Song

Like pain of fire runs down my body my love to you, my
    dear!
Like pain runs down my body my love to you, my dear!
Just as sickness is my love to you, my dear.
Just as a boil pains me my love to you, my dear.
Just as fire burns me my love to you, my dear.
I am thinking of what you said to me.
I am thinking of the love you bear me.
I am afraid of your love, my dear.
O pain! O pain!
Oh, where is my true love going, my dear?
Oh, they say she will be taken away far from here. She will
    leave me, my true love, my dear.
My body feels numb on account of what I said, my true love,
    my dear.
Good-bye, my true love, my dear.

KWAKIUTL

Woman's Song

A loon
I thought it was
But it was
My love's
Splashing oar

To Sault Ste. Marie
He has departed
My love
Has gone on before me
Never again
Can I see him

CHIPPEWA

Clear River

Clear river
of the *llámran* trees,
tears from fish of gold,
tears from great cliffs.

Deep river
of the *tara* groves,
lost at the chasm's bend,
screaming in a chasm of parrots.

Dear river,
carry me and my young love
far, far, past rocks
and into rainclouds.

QUECHUA

Song

Early morning dawning green,
Ah . . . is the willow so green?
In the green fields,
You gave me your love.

QUECHUA

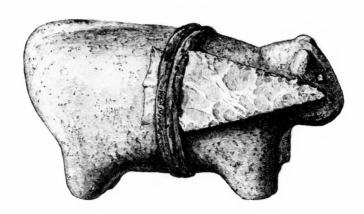

For the Traveler

Zuni fetish representing the
mountain lion, used for safe
passage through enemy country
(*2d An. Rep. of the Bur. of Amer.*
Ethnology).

Life Song

This is my heart as I travel all over; my spirit, my life and
   living.

FLATHEAD

Traveler's Prayer, with an Offering of Copal

O God, O lord of the mountains and valleys, I have offered you a bit of your food, your drink. And now I continue on, beneath your feet and your hands, I, a traveler.

It cannot hurt you, it cannot grieve you to give me plenty of game, big game, small game, O my father. For you have much. You have trogons, pheasants, boars. Show them, reveal them. Take them and set them in my path.

I will see them and find them, for I am beneath your feet, beneath your hands: I am fortunate, O lord of the mountains, O lord of the valleys. By your will, your name, and your being, all things are abundant. May I share in them all.

Today, perhaps, I must eat my tortillas, and yet I am in rich hunting lands. I hope God can see that there are no living creatures about. Perhaps I will get, perhaps I will catch just one little trogon.

I will see it, I will find it, O God, O Mother, O Father. This is my word and my thought. Though what I have brought along for you to eat, for you to drink, is neither good nor much, nevertheless my words, my thoughts, are these, O Mother, O Father.

Now I will sleep beneath your feet, beneath your hands, O lord of the mountains and valleys, O lord of the trees, O lord of the creeping vines. Again tomorrow there will be day, again tomorrow there will be light. I know not where I will be.

Who is my mother? Who is my father? Only you, O God.
You watch me, guard me, on every path, through every
darkness, and before each obstacle that you might hide
or take away, O God, my lord, O lord of the mountains
and valleys.

My words, my thoughts, are these. I may have said too
much, or not enough. You will endure, you will forgive,
my error.

KEKCHI MAYA

Prayer to the Sun, for Quick Travel

Sun, come help me.
I'll be first, I'll go first.
Then you, then you can go.
I'll be the first to reach the end
of all the desert lands,
of all the canyon lands,
passing over the earth's smooth face.
Smooth or not smooth,
she'll never hurt me.
Right through the sky I'll go.
That's where I'll be.

AZTEC

To Make the Road Seem Short

Now! Leech, quickly You have just come undulating in!

Now! Leech, quickly You have just come in and balled
yourself up!

Now! Leech, quickly You have just come in and compressed
yourself into a mass!

Now! Hummingbird, quickly You have just come to help me
go! *Dayi!*

CHEROKEE

Prayer for Safe Passage Through Enemy Country

/ *The warrior opens his pouch, takes out his fetish, and scatters a pinch or two of prayer meal toward each of the four quarters. He holds the fetish in his left hand over his heart and kneels or squats on the ground, praying:* /

Now!
This day,
My fathers,
Divine ones,
Here in this land,
Filled with enemies,
Make me precious.
That in any way, even unexpectedly,
No enemy may dare to strike me,
This day,
For me,
Make me a shield.

/ *With the edge of an arrowhead lashed to the fetish, he scratches or cuts in the earth a line about six inches long.* /

That none may pass through,
No enemy, none whatsoever,
Make me a shield.

/ *He scratches a second line.* /

Mountain Lion!

/ *Scratches a third line.* /

Knife Wing!

/ *A fourth line.* /

May you shield my heart.

/ *He breathes on the fetish and replaces it in the pouch.* /

ZUNI

71

Salt Pilgrimage

This is the story of my desire
There was my wife's cooking that I didn't carefully eat
My child that I didn't carefully hold
"What does he know that he acts this way?"
Through this my days were completed and so I could go.

Done, I emerged and stepped on the west lying road
Someplace got tired and evening came
Then took my burning stick
Made a fire and towards it bent over and sat.
In my bag reached and took my reed cigarette
Stood it and puffed it, breathed on the west lying road
Asked for the man, my made father,
Asked for different kinds of strength
Hungerness, thirstness, coldness, strong carrying legs, strong
      arms, clear eyes.

Four times spilled the coming dawn and again I stepped on
      the west lying road
Then reached the man, my made father.
Strongly to me he did.
The white mixture he put, the white clay likeness, with it on
      my chest he really marked, on my back he marked me,
      on my shoulder blades both sides he marked me

Then very well blew on me and did to me
So I would never feel things while going around.
Thus you may wish, my various relatives.

PAPAGO

Songs of the Horse Society

1

Daybreak
appears
when
a horse
neighs

2

Friend
my horse
flies like a bird
as it runs

SIOUX

It Starts Toward Me

The beautiful thing is starting toward me
I being son of the sun
The white-shell bead horse is starting toward me
From the center of the sun's home it is starting toward me
It eats out of the white-shell basket
The dark clouds' dew streams from it as it starts toward me
The pollen from the beautiful flowers streams from its
    mouth as it starts toward me
With its beautiful neigh it calls as it starts toward me
Soft goods of all sorts are attached to it as it starts toward me
Hard goods of all sorts are attached to it as it starts toward
    me
It shall continue to increase without fail as it starts toward
    me
It shall be beautiful in front of it as it starts toward me
It shall be beautiful behind it as it starts toward me
Good and everlasting one am I as it starts toward me.

NAVAJO

Against Sickness and Evil

Huichol shaman's "plume of the sun" with rattlesnake rattler attached, used for brushing the patient's body (*Memoirs of the Amer. Mus. of Nat. Hist., vol. 3*).

To Blow Away a Headache

Father Kumu, you magician, I've done it! There in the medicine hut I made myself drunk.
O phantom man, don't be my child! Don't be this sickness
soaring in my head!
Without a glance at this child—and as soon as you came—in
the medicine hut I prepared the sweet herb and blew
you away with my breath.

UITOTO

For Chest Pain

/ The medicine woman applies crushed tobacco and anise to the patient's chest, with these words: /

Come, nine-times-powdered ones, nine-times-crushed ones.
And you, green pain, dark pain,
are you such a master, such a great one
that you hurt this man?
Chase it away, go to it, you precious ones.
Where does it lie?
In my spiritual rib cage, my spiritual backbone.
Come in through my spiritual head.
Don't be shy, you spirits,
you five times lucky ones, you yellow women.

AZTEC

To Cure Epilepsy

Green fire, mist in the air,
you have changed yourself into epilepsy.
Yellow fire, you have changed yourself into epilepsy.
North wind,
you have changed yourself into epilepsy,
epilepsy caused by a dream,
white mist, you have changed yourself into epilepsy,
red mist, you have changed yourself into epilepsy.
We will undo it,
nine times we will undo it,
we will undo it,
nine times we will undo it,
we will relieve it, nine times relieve it, Lord.
In an hour, a half hour, to be gone like a mist,
to be gone like a butterfly.
Adjust yourself, great pulse! Adjust yourself, little pulse!
Both pulses in an hour, a half hour,
thus may it be, Lord.
Now come to an end
upon thirteen mountains,
upon thirteen ridges,
now come to an end amid thirteen rows of rocks,
now come to an end amid thirteen rows of trees.

TZOTZIL MAYA

From a Prayer of the Shooting Chant

May evil sorcery be given the wink
May the evils of sorcery be driven off in crowds
May evil sorcery sail off like a feather
May evil sorcery be filed down
May the weapon of evil sorcery withered move away
    from me.

NAVAJO

Confession of Sin

/ *The sorcerer speaks to the fire on behalf of the sinner:* /

Mother of gods, father of gods, Ancient God,
A mere appendage of the realm, a common man, has come.
He comes crying, he comes in sadness, he comes with guilt.
Perhaps he has slipped, perhaps he has stumbled, perhaps he
    has touched the bird of evil, the spider's web, the tuft of
    thorns:
It wounds his heart, it troubles him.
Master, Lord,
Ever Present, Ever Near,
Take it from him: hear the pain of this common man.

/ *The sinner speaks:* /

Lord, Ever Present, Ever Near,
Take it from me, hear my stench, my corruption.
I undress to your face, I show my nakedness.
The act was mine, I did it.
Can what I have done in your presence be secret? Can it be
    in darkness? No, it is mirrored, it is in the light.

AZTEC

83

Prayer to the Migratory Birds

Welcome, Supernatural Ones, we have come to meet alive,
    friends, you, Long-Life-Makers.
You have come and I pray you again that you have mercy
    and take out again this my sickenss when you go back to
    the place where you always disappear, friends.
Now protect me again during the time when you are here in
    summer in this good country where I treat you well,
    Long-Life-Makers, Supernatural Ones.

Then the man himself replies to his words, on behalf of the birds. He says:

Hâ, I will do this.

KWAKIUTL

Magic Words to the Gull

The gull, it is said,
The one who cleaves the air with its wings,
The one that is usually above you.
Hò-he, aya.
Hò-he, aya.
Gull, you up there,
Steer down towards me,
Come to me.
Your wings
Are red,
Up there in the coolness.
Aya-ya,
Aya-ya.

NETSILIK ESKIMO

A Song of the Coyoteway

The Furs are put in the water.
Black Lightning is put in the body.
Male Rain is there.
Black Water is there.
Crystal Rock is there.
In the wide Land I walk.

The Black Fur is put in the rainbow.
It is put in the Black Water.
The White Crystal is there.
Roads to the wide Land I walk.
The Holy Black Cloud is there.
Crystal Rock is there.
In the Black Water I walk.

To the Beautiful Place I walk.
In the Country of Water I walk.
Furs put into Corn-pollen,
And beautiful Water is there.

NAVAJO

Dream Songs

1

As a head only, I roll around.

2

I stand on the rim of my nest.

3

I am enveloped in flames.

4

What am I? What am I?

5

I, the song, I walk here.

MODOC

Medicine Man's Prayer

Listen, my dream!
This you told me should be done.
This you said should be the way.
You said it would cure the sick.
Help me now.
Do not lie to me.
Help me, Sun person.
Help me to cure this sick man.

BLACKFEET

I Am the Medicine

I am the medicine
I am the damp herb
Come back lost spirit
I will whistle to guide you

/ *He whistles* /

Return!
May there come with you
Thirteen deer
Thirteen eagles
Thirteen white horses
Thirteen rainbows
Your steps move thirteen mountains
The big clown is calling you
The master clown is calling you
I will make the mountains resound
I will make their abysses resound
I will make the dawn resound
I will make the day resound

MAZATEC

Medicine Songs

1

Sunrise
may you behold

2

A dawn
appears
behold it

SIOUX

Morning Prayer to the Creator

O true Spirit Father! First One!

Upon your earth the Great-Heart Spirit now appears: the sacred eye!

O Provider, you willed it that we waken, and we have wakened.

And as we wake, though we are few in number and far removed from you, we say these sacred words that never die.

Again and again because of these you let us waken.

O true Spirit Father! First One!

MBYÁ

Controlling the Weather

Chippewa hawk-leg fetish, used
for appeasing the thunder spirit
(*7th An. Rep. of the Bur. of Amer.
Ethnology*).

To Quiet a Raging Storm

Man outside,
please come in,
please enter into me.

COPPER ESKIMO

Magic Spell for an
Approaching Storm

Against the great darkness looming up armed,
I am falling,
into its center, falling,
displacing it to the highest hill,
up vast slopes, carrying it,
pressing it down on the cap of the hill.

AREKUNA

This Is to Frighten a Storm

Yuhahí, yuhahí, yuhahí, yuhahí, yuhahí,
Yuhahí, yuhahí, yuhahí, yuhahí, yuhahí—Yû!
Listen! O now you are coming in rut. Ha! I am exceedingly
    afraid of you. But yet you are only tracking your wife.
    Her footprints can be seen there, directed upward to-
    ward the heavens. I have pointed them out for you. Let
    your paths stretch out along the treetops on the lofty
    mountains. You shall have them—the paths—lying
    down without being disturbed. Let your path as you go
    along be where the waving branches meet. Listen!

CHEROKEE

Girl's Prayer to Thunder
During a Storm

Do not harm us! If you have a son, I will marry him.

BLACKFEET

Song for Smooth Waters

Ocean Spirit
calm the waves for me
get close to me, my power
my heart is tired
make the sea like milk for me
yeho
yehólo

HAIDA

Boatman's Prayer for Smooth Waters

Old Man, put your hands on the sea and press it down!

KWAKIUTL

Prayer for Smooth Waters

Be gracious to me, my Father, hold up the boat.

YAHGAN

Song

Don't you ever
you up in the sky
don't you ever get tired
of having the clouds
between you and us?

NOOTKA

Weather Incantation

Cold, Cold,
Frost, Frost,
Fling me not aside!
You have bent me enough.
Away! Away!

IGLULIK ESKIMO

Song for Calling Rain

Great bubble-eyed one,
rain owner,
hayē.

KWAKIUTL

Thunder Song

Thonah! Thonah!
There is a voice above,
The voice of the thunder.
Within the dark cloud,
Again and again it sounds,
Thonah! Thonah!

Thonah! Thonah!
There is a voice below,
The voice of the grasshopper.
Among the plants,
Again and again it sounds,
Thonah! Thonah!

NAVAJO

Special Request for the
Children of Mother Corn

Perhaps if we are lucky
Our earth mother
Will wrap herself in a fourfold robe
Of white meal,
Full of frost flowers;
A floor of ice will spread over the world,
The forests,
Because of the cold, will lean to one side,
Their arms will break beneath the weight of snow.
When the days are thus,
The flesh of our earth mother
Will crack with cold.
Then in the spring when she is replete with living waters,
Our mothers,
All different kinds of corn,
In their earth mother
We shall lay to rest.
With their earth mother's living waters
They will be made into new beings;
Into their sun father's daylight
They will come out standing;
Yonder to all directions
They will stretch out their hands calling for rain.
Then with their fresh waters
[The rain makers] will pass us on our roads.

Clasping their young ones in their arms,
They will rear their children.
Gathering them into our houses,
Following these toward whom our thoughts bend,
With our thoughts following them,
Thus we shall always live.

ZUNI

Planting and Gathering

Hopi mask representing the fe-
male form of the spirit *Pawíkka-
tcina* (*15th An. Rep. of the Bur. of
Amer. Ethnology*).

Song

Our mother of the growing fields, our mother of the streams,
    will have pity upon us.
For to whom do we belong? Whose seeds are we? To our
    mother alone do we belong.

CÁGABA

Prayer Before Felling to
Clear a Cornfield

O God, my mother, my father, lord of the hills, lord of the
    valleys, lord of the forest, be patient with me. I am
    about to do as has always been done.

Now I make you an offering, that you may be warned: I am
    about to molest your heart. Perhaps you will have the
    strength to endure it.

I am going to dirty you, I am going to work you in order that
    I may live.

Let no animal pursue me, no snake, no scorpion, no wasp
    annoy me, no falling timber hit me, no ax, no machete
    catch me.

With all my heart I am going to work you.

KEKCHI MAYA

Prayer

They have cleared away the place where the corn is to be
    planted; they have planted it; the ground grows damp;
    it begins to grow; now the work is done.
The corn will give me strength; I will conquer the enemy.
Chief, make everything grow.
My Mother has done her work: the corn is growing; the
    leaves are spreading out; I see the enemy.
We are strong.
The corn is ripening.

ARIKARA

A Song of the Corn Dance

Hí híanai hu!
Here on my field
Corn comes forth.
My child takes it and runs,
Happy.

Here on my field
Squash comes forth.
My wife takes it and runs,
Singing.

PAPAGO

Songs of the Corn Dance

1

Among the flowers I am moving reverently.

2

Among the flowers I am singing, dancing.

3

Berries ripen,
Fruit ripens.

SENECA

To Keep Animals Out
of the Cornfield

/ Fire and incense are brought to the edge of the field, and any broken stalks or ears of corn spoiled by animals are destroyed. Throwing incense into the fire, the speaker begins: /

I am the wizard jaguar,
I have come to find my uncles, the spirits,
the yellow spirits, the brown spirits.
Ah, here they come,
here they are,
and off they go.
I've come to follow them.
They won't eat here again.
I'll send them off.
They'll run away.
I bring white incense, yellow incense,
and with it I deprive my uncles, the spirits,
the yellow spirits, the brown spirits.

/ More incense is offered, with these words addressed to the fire: /

My father, 4 Reed, Flaming One!

AZTEC

Harvester's Prayer, with an
Offering of Copal

O God, my lord, Mother, Father, lord of the mountains and
    valleys.
Now and in just three suns, in just three days, before your
    mouth and before your face, I will start to gather my
    corn, O lord of the mountains and valleys. Now show
    my soul and body how to find it.
I give you a little of what you eat, of what you drink. It
    amounts to nothing, this offering to you. And yet what I
    eat myself, what I drink myself, is plenty and good. You
    have shown it to my soul and body, you my mother, you
    my father.
And so I start my harvest, before your mouth, before your
    face.
But it will not be done in one day. Who knows how many
    suns, how many days I will harvest? The gathering can-
    not go quickly among the weeds. Only if I do it slowly
    can I do it well.
Who knows when I will be able to speak to you again, O
    Mother, O Father, O angel, O lord of the mountains
    and valleys. Will I pray to you again? Why not, O God?

KEKCHI MAYA

Prayer to the Corn Mothers

Our old women gods, we ask you!
Our old women gods, we ask you!
Then give us long life together,
May we live until our frosted hair
Is white; may we live till then
This life that now we know!

TEWA

Prayer Before Eating

Our father, hear us, and our grandfather. I mention also all
those that shine, the yellow day, the good wind, the
good timber, and the good earth.

All the animals, listen to me under the ground. Animals
above ground, and water animals, listen to me. We shall
eat your remnants of food. Let them be good.

Let there be long breath and life. Let the people increase, the
children of all ages, the girls and the boys, and the men
of all ages and the women, the old men of all ages and
the old women. The food will give us strength whenever
the sun runs.

Listen to us, Father, Grandfather. We ask thought, heart,
love, happiness. We are going to eat.

ARAPAHO

Prayer Before the First Meal
in a New Summer Camp

We are glad to be here.

We are going to give our food to this our country.

Make us strong; make us lucky.

Keep the women in good health so that they may dig camas
and other roots in plenty for the winter.

Sun, you give us what we want so that we may be happy.

Sun, you are all-knowing. You want us to have a good time
and to live well.

Now, great sun, you know everything because you are over
us.

MODOC

Prayer to the Sun

Sun, my relative, be good coming out.
Do something good for us.

Make me work,
So I can do anything I wish in the garden.
I hoe, I plant corn, I irrigate.

You, sun, be good going down at sunset.
We lie down to sleep. I want to feel good.
While I sleep, you come up.

Go on your course many times.
Make good things for us men.
Make me always the same as I am now.

HAVASUPAI

For the Hunter

Eskimo fetish representing a
hunter, used for controlling the
movements of game animals
(*11th An. Rep. of the Bur. of Amer.
Ethnology*).

Offering to Deceased Hunters

Here, grandfathers, eat! And whoever had good luck in
hunting lend me your hand and your thoughts.

ZUNI

A Song of the Buffalo Dance

There one comes
one comes standing
there one comes
one comes standing
quietly standing
waiting for the sun

PAWNEE

A Song of the Buffalo Dance

In the north
the wind
blows
they are walking
the hail
beats
they are walking

SIOUX

A Song of the Buffalo Dance

One I have wounded, yonder he moves,
Yonder he moves, bleeding at the mouth.

One I have wounded, yonder he moves,
Yonder he moves, with staggering steps.

One I have wounded, yonder he moves,
Yonder he falls, yonder he falls.

OMAHA

Prayer to the Black Bear

When the black bear is dead, when it has been shot by the hunter, the man sits down on the ground at the right-hand side of the bear. Then the man says, praying to it,

Thank you, friend, that you did not make me walk about in
    vain.

Now you have come to take mercy on me so that I obtain
    game, that I may inherit your power of getting easily
    with your hands the salmon that you catch.

Now I will press my right hand against your left hand

—says the man as he takes hold of the left paw of the bear. He says,

O friend, now we press together our working hands, that you
    may give over to me your power of getting everything
    easily with your hands, friend

—says he. Now it is done after this, for now he only skins the bear after this.

KWAKIUTL

129

Words to Call Up Game

Beast of the sea,
Come and offer yourself in the dear early morning!
Beast of the plain,
Come and offer yourself in the dear early morning!

IGLULIK ESKIMO

Prayer to the Whale

Whale, I want you to come near me, so that I will get hold of
    your heart and deceive it, so that I will have strong legs
    and not be trembling and excited when the whale
    comes and I spear him.

Whale, you must not run out to sea when I spear you.

Whale, if I spear you, I want my spear to strike your heart.
    Harpoon, when I use you, I want you to go to the heart
    of the whale.

Whale, when I spear at you and miss you, I want you to take
    hold of my spear with your hands.

Whale, do not break my canoe, for I am going to do good to
    you. I am going to put eagle-down and cedar-bark on
    your back.

Whale, if I use only one canoe to kill you, I want to kill you
    dead.

NOOTKA

For Subduing a Walrus

The walrus, I harpoon it,
Stroking its cheek.
You have become quiet and meek.
The walrus, I harpoon it,
Patting its tusks.
You have become quiet and meek.

AMMASSALIK ESKIMO

Eagle Song

An eagle is walking,
Toward me it is walking.
Its long feathers blow in the breeze.

A hawk is running,
Toward me it is running.
Its down feathers ruffle in the wind.

PAPAGO

Prayer Before Killing an Eagle

Do not think I shall harm you.
You will have a new body.
Now turn your head to the north and lie flat!

YOKUTS

Before Butchering the Deer

Yes, my wish was done

There was the thick straw, with it a person I made and finished it

There were the rainbows, I made them be hind legs

There was the milky way, I made it be forelegs

There was the wind, I rubbed it all over, then [the deer that
was being made] dripped [water]

There was the thick straw, I put it on the head [as horns]

There were the broad leaves, I put them on it as ears

And the wind I folded, put it on it as a snout

There was the hail, I made it into eyes

There was the wind, I rubbed it all over, then it dripped

And there was the cloud, I put it on it for buttocks and
pressed it

Then I made hair for it and let it go.

There was a mountain, over its black rocks [the deer]
jumped and in front of it danced, and behind a grey
mountain it stood.

Behind that stood a flowering tree

Behind that were my grown boys, they threw it down and
wounded it

Then ran up my old man, my boy, my child, they rubbed
themselves with [the tail of the deer], they asked for a
good life.

PAPAGO

135

Prayer to a Dead Buck

In the future that we may continue to hold each other with
    the turquoise hand
Now that you may return to the place from which you came
In the future as time goes on that I may rely on you for food
To the home of the dawn you are starting to return
With the jet hoofs you are starting to return
By means of the zigzag lightning you are starting to return
By the evening twilight your legs are yellow
That way you are starting to return
By the white of dawn your buttocks are white and that way
    you are starting to return
A dark tail is in your tail and that way you are starting to
    return
A haze is in your fur and that way you are starting to return
A growing vegetation is in your ears and that way you are
    starting to return
A mixture of beautiful flowers and water is in your intestines
    and that way you are starting to return
May turquoise be in your liver and abalone shell the parti-
    tion between your heart and intestines and that way
    you are starting to return
May red shell be your lungs and white shell be your wind-
    pipe and that way you are starting to return
May dark wind and straight lightning be your speech and
    that way you are starting to return
There you have returned within the interior of the jet basket
    in the midst of the beautiful flower pollens

Beautifully you have arrived home

Beautifully may you and I both continue to live

From this day may you lead the other game along the trails,
that I may hunt.

Because I have obeyed all the restrictions laid down by your
god in hunting and skinning you

Therefore I ask for this luck: that I may continue to have
good luck in hunting you.

NAVAJO

A Prayer of the Midwinter Hunt

/ The hunter proceeds to the House of the Deer Medicine, where a basket containing fetishes is placed before him by the Keeper. Facing in the direction belonging to the particular fetish he intends to use, the hunter sprinkles prayer meal over the basket. Then, holding a small quantity of the meal in his left hand over his heart, he removes his headband and prays: /

Indeed,
This day,
My father,
My mother,
Unexpectedly I have passed you on your road.
For my fathers,
Dance priests,
Beast priests,
Divine ones,
With whatever plume wands I have prepared,
Bringing plume wands for them,
I have passed you on your road.
With prayer meal,
Desiring your children,
Upon my earth mother
Yonder with prayers,
I will make my road go out.
Over all the land,
Your children,
The deer,
Obeying your breath,
Go wandering.
Desiring their flesh,

Their blood,
Yonder with prayers
I will make my road go out.
Let it be without fail
That you grant me your children,
That you make me happy,
That you bless me with light.

/ Scattering prayer meal in the direction he proposes to take, he chooses his fetish and, pressing it to his lips, breathes from it, saying: /

Ah!
Thanks,
My father,
My mother.
This day,
Following your road,
Yonder with prayers,
I will make my road go out.

ZUNI

For the Dying and the Dead

Arara war trophy (*Bur. of Amer. Ethnology Bul. 143, vol. 3*).

Song

The world is rolling around for all the young people, so let's not love our life too much, hold ourselves back from dying.

TLINGIT

Chief's Song

I will sing the song of the sky.
Now this is the owl flying downward, circling,
tired of all songs,
the salmon where the swift current moves circling,
runs circling.
Their call is urgent.
The sky turns over.
They are calling for me.

TSIMSHIAN

Song of Farewell to the Deceased

Where are you going, my father?
I am going to the great forest, I am going walking.
Why do you go? Who goes with you?
I go to harvest the sweet coca leaf, I go alone.
Come back soon, come back soon.
I will wait for you crying,
I will wait for you grieving.

In the woods where you must go
A black flag is waving.
In the open place that you must cross
The parting grass spreads cloaks of flowers.
What heart is this bitter heart
That leaves the dove?

Little bell of Paucartambo,
Ring farewell for me.
I am going to the great forest.
I will never return.

QUECHUA

Crazy-Dog Prayer

You Above, if there be one there who knows what is going
    on, repay me today for the distress I have suffered.
Inside the Earth, if there be anyone there who knows what is
    going on, repay me for the distress I have suffered.
The One Who Causes Things, whoever he be, I have now
    had my fill of life.
Grant me death, my sorrows are overabundant.
Though children are timid, they die harsh deaths, it is said.
    Though women are timid, you make them die harsh
    deaths.
I do not want to live long; were I to live long, my sorrows
    would be overabundant. I do not want it!

CROW

Crazy-Dog Song

I live, but I cannot live forever.
Only the great earth lives forever,
the great sun is the only living thing.

KIOWA

A Widow's Lament

It was in the night that I awoke, I, the woman, looking for
the founder of my nation, my lord, the precious man,
the man I love. And where do I hear him? Ah, the noble
lord goes song-weeping at Ocotepec. They've seized him
in the scuffle, at the gorge. In the Crimson now I seek
you.

Ah, I'm grieving at my fireside, picking red feather-flowers.
For you. Have you reached the Shore, the Water's-
Spreading-Out-Place? Pass away adorned with these
bereavement flowers that are yours. I seek you.

AZTEC

Song of a Ghost

From the old camping place
Comes a flash of flowers.
I love flowers.
Give me flowers.
Flowers flutter
As the wind raises them above.
I love flowers.
Give me flowers.

WINTU

Song of Two Ghosts

My friend
this is a wide world
We're traveling over
Walking on the moonlight

OMAHA

Prayer to the Ghost

Here it is, the tobacco. I am certain that you, O ghost, are
   not very far away, that in fact you are standing right in
   back of me, waiting for me to reach you the pipe and
   tobacco, that you might take it along with you, that
   likewise you are waiting for your food to take on your
   journey. However, four nights you will have to remain
   here.

Now here are these things, and in return we ask you to act as
   mediator [between the spirits and us]. You have made
   us long for you, and therefore see to it that all those
   things that belonged to you and that you would have
   enjoyed had you lived longer—victories on the warpath,
   earthly possessions, and life—that all these things you
   leave behind for us to enjoy. This you must ask for us as
   you travel along.

This also I ask of you: do not cause us to follow you soon; do
   not cause your brothers any fear.

I have now lit the pipe for you.

WINNEBAGO

Prayer to the Deceased

My child, you have toiled through life and come to the end
of suffering: and now our lord has obliged you.

Truly our home is not on earth: only for a while, only briefly
do we warm ourselves in the sun; and only as our lord
wills it do we enjoy the companionship of one another.

You have been taken in by the Dead Land Lord, He of the
Swirling Waters, He of the Headlong Descent, and also
the Dead Land Lady.

He has made you be his servant, he has made you be his seat.
For truly our home is there, our place of destruction is
there, there where the earth grows wide, where it all
ends.

Now you have gone, gone to whatever kind of place it may
be, the place where all are shorn, the place we all go to,
the place of no lights and no windows, never again to
return, to come back. You will think no more of what
lies here, of what lies behind you.

At the end of many days you went away and left your children, your grandchildren; you left them ophaned, you
left them living. You will think no more of what may
become of them.

We will go and join you, we will go be with you at the end of
many days.

AZTEC

152

Prayer to the Deceased

We have muddied the waters for you,
We have cast shadows between us,
We have made steep gullies between us,
Do not, therefore, reach for even a hair of our heads,
Rather, help us attain that which we are always seeking,
Long life, that our children may grow,
Abundant game, the raising of crops,
And in all the works of man
Ask for these things for all, and do no more,
And now you must go, for now you are free.

TEWA

Prayer to the Deceased

Naked you came from Earth the Mother. Naked you return
to her. May a good wind be your road.

OMAHA

References given by author or by author and short title can be located in the Sources following the Notes.

Introduction

Page 5 / Sir Edward B. Tylor's: Tylor, *Primitive culture,* 7th ed. (1924), vol. 2, p. 364. *Language of spells is virtually unknown to the . . . Plains tribes:* for an exception, see the Arikara prayer on p. 113. *From the Chippewa:* see p. 43. *From the Modoc:* see p. 87.

Page 6 / "May you live until your hair is white": compare the Tewa prayer on p. 118. *"May you fall asleep old":* compare the Hopi prayer on p. 21. *"Soft words":* Ruth Underhill, *Singing for Power,* University of California Press, 1968, p. 112. *"May your road reach to Dawn Lake":* see p. 41. *"Sacred path":* Joseph Epes Brown, *The Sacred Pipe,* University of Oklahoma Press, 1953, pp. 37, 41, 120.

Birth and Infancy

Page 13 / Translated from the Navajo by Berard Haile, in Wyman, p. 337. Part of a ceremony called "expelling the child." The prayer is recited by the chanter, or medicine man, and repeated by the woman in labor, phrase by phrase. If a boy is desired, the word "boy" is substituted for "girl." Only a portion of the full prayer is given here—but in practice, if the labor is difficult and the woman is unable to repeat long prayers, no more than a portion can be used. *Pollen Girl . . . Cornbeetle Girl:* The mother identifies her baby with the deities Pollen Boy and Cornbeetle Girl, Navajo spirits of blessing and protectiveness (see Gladys Reichard, *Navaho Religion,* Pantheon, 1963, p. 457).

Page 14 / Translated from the Arekuna by Cesáreo de Armellada, p. 159

(the English version is mine, after the Spanish of Armellada). One of over a hundred magic spells, or *tarén,* collected by Armellada before 1966. A complete *tarén* consists of a "song," or chant, preceded by an explanatory myth and followed by the name of the mythical character who is supposed to have uttered it. Only the chant itself is given here. The native informant advised Armellada: "This is the *tarén* that is spoken over the woman's belly. Collect this *tarén* in order to use it with your women, blowing on their head and on their belly."

Page 15 / Translated from the Eskimo by William Thalbitzer, p. 499. A "petting song," sung to the child as an expression of maternal happiness.

Page 16 / Translated from the Kwakiutl by Franz Boas, in his *Kwakiutl Ethnography,* p. 346. Kwakiutl songs to young children generally express hopes for the future. As a token of affection, the parent may refer to himself as the "slave" and the child as his "master."

Page 17 / Translated from the Kwakiutl by Franz Boas, in his *Religion of the Kwakiutl Indians,* pt. 2, p. 202. The birth of twins is an event filled with significance and attended by literally dozens of restrictions. Twins are believed to have power over weather, disease, and salmon fishing (see Boas, *Kwakiutl Ethnography,* pp. 365–68). *You who come from the sea:* Twins of the same sex are thought to be salmon that have assumed human form. *Rich-Makers:* because they can call the salmon.

Page 18 / My translation of the Aztec text in Sahagún, bk. 6, ch. 32. As soon as the midwife has cut the umbilical cord, she prepares to bathe the child, reciting this prayer to Chalchiuhtlicue ("Jade Skirt"), the goddess of water. When the prayer is finished, she breathes on the water, makes the baby taste it, touches a little of it to the baby's head and chest, and, finally, bathes and swaddles him (or her). *Two Lord, Two Lady:* sometimes translated "Lord of Duality, Lady of Duality," the mythic source of life. *Ancient night:* literally, "night place"; possibly refers to a mythic time before the creation of the sun.

Page 20 / Translated from the Eskimo by Knud Rasmussen, in his *Iglu-*

lik Eskimos, p. 47 (translated from Rasmussen's Danish into English by W. Worster). Rasmussen writes: "The sledges were piled with goods to the height of a man, and just as we were about to start, I had the opportunity of seeing how a newborn infant enters upon its first sledge journey. A hole was cut in the wall from within at the back of Kublo's house, and his wife crawled out through it with her little daughter in her arms. Then she stood in front of the snow hut, waiting, and Aua, who as the *angákoq* had to see that all needful rites were properly observed, went up to the child, bared its head, and with his lips close to its face . . . introduced [the child] to life by means of the magic formula here given."

Page 21 / Translated from the Hopi by H. R. Voth, p. 53. At dawn on the fifth day after the birth of a daughter, the mother, if she is well enough, or her mother or her mother-in-law, goes out to the edge of the village and recites this prayer with an offering of meal. If the child is a boy, "old men" is substituted for "old women." Evidently the "we" refers to the child only.

Page 22 / Translated from the Tewa by Herbert J. Spinden, p. 106. *Godmother:* probably the "umbilical cord-cutting mother" mentioned by Alfonso Ortiz, pp. 29–33. *Rain-dew Falling . . . Star Mountain:* Spinden notes that a child may receive more than one name; according to Ortiz, the name may be inspired by some natural phenomenon observed at the time of the ritual (which takes place the fourth day after birth).

Page 23 / Translated from the Kiowa, in Natalie Curtis, pp. 239 and 547. A "stop-crying song."

Page 24 / Translated from the Mbyá by León Cadogan, p. 180 (the English version is mine, after the Spanish of Cadogan).

Page 25 / My translation from the Aztec, in Bierhorst, *Cantares Mexicanos,* song 57, stanzas 7–8. Excerpted from a thirty-stanza satirical song summoning the ghost of the deceased king Ahuitzotl. The underlying idea is that the singer will bring Ahuitzotl back to earth as a newborn. In the two stanzas given here, we have what appears to be a parody of a genuine Aztec lullaby.

Page 26 / Translated from the Creek, in Rhodes, "Indian Songs of Today." Another lullaby promising the father's return. Compare the songs on pp. 24 and 25, above.

Page 27 / Translated from the Eskimo by Knud Rasmussen, in his *Iglulik Eskimos,* p. 167 (translated from Rasmussen's Danish into English by W. Worster).

Growing Up

Page 31 / Translated from the Zuni by Ruth Bunzel, in her "Zuñi Katcinas," p. 854. At every meal some woman of the house will go into the room where the dancing masks are kept and present them with an offering of food. Sometimes for good luck the youngest daughter will be told to go in and feed these "grandfathers."

Page 32 / Translated from the Arapaho by A. L. Kroeber, in his *Arapaho,* p. 313. Excerpted from a longer prayer. Among the Arapaho it is said that a boy takes his new name and "goes away." The old name "stays here." (The giving of a new name at puberty is a widespread Indian custom.) *Those that shine above at night:* the stars.

Page 33 / Translated from the Sioux by Benjamin Black Elk (son of Black Elk) and revised by J. G. Neihardt, p. 243. Recited for the benefit of the Sioux mystic, Black Elk, during the Ghost Dance activity of 1890.

Page 34 / Translated from the Crow, in E. S. Curtis, vol. 4, p. 53. The young man fasts alone in the wilderness, waiting for a vision. He calls out to the principal spirit, He That Hears Always, and to all the lesser spirits, one of whom, he hopes, will speak to him and become his helper. *A fingertip:* During the vision quest a Crow "usually cut off a finger joint of his left hand or in some other way mortified his flesh by way of arousing supernatural pity" (Robert H. Lowie, *Indians of the Plains,* Natural History Press, 1963, p. 170).

Page 35 / Translated from the Cherokee by J. F. and A. G. Kilpatrick, in their *Walk in Your Soul,* pp. 86–87. The seven-part structure of this magic spell makes it especially powerful. The young man, in private, recites it four times, concluding each recitation by blowing his breath toward the place where the young woman of his choice is believed to be at that moment. In the third line he speaks his clan name and his personal name. *Seven Clans:* the Cherokee nation.

Page 36 / Translated from the Apache by P. E. Goddard, in his *Jicarilla Apache Texts,* pp. 266–67. A girl at puberty emulates the great goddess of Apache mythology, called White-Shell Woman. A boy representing Child of the Water, the mythical son of White-Shell Woman, partici- pates in the ceremony, presumably in order to bring good luck in child- bearing. *White-Painted Woman:* another name for White-Shell Woman. *Jewel dust:* The Apache term is *l'eshtchic* (compare Navajo *t'estchich*), which Goddard does not translate; evidently it is a powdered form of sparkling rock (see Clyde Kluckhohn and L. C. Wyman, *An Introduction to Navaho Chant Practice,* Memoirs of the American Anthropological Asso- ciation, no. 53, 1940, p. 25); both the jewel dust and the pollen are of- ferings, or, as one might say, unspoken prayers, symbolizing light and life. *On top of my feet:* as though walking ankle-deep in pollen.

Page 37 / Translated from the Apache by P. E. Goddard, in his "Masked Dancers of the Apache," p. 133. *Dancers:* literally, *gahe* chil- dren, the masked dancers who impersonate the *gahe* spirits and whose performance is a standard feature of Apache girls' puberty ceremonies. *Mescal Mountain:* the mythical home of the gahe, where Douglas spruce grows.

Page 38 / Translated from the Apache by Claire R. Farrer, p. 145. Refers to the footrace connected with the girls' puberty ceremony. Na- vajo and Apache girls, when they reach puberty, dress in their finest clothes and undergo a four days' ritual, which includes fasting, singing, a massage to make the girl's body beautiful, and a special footrace that the girl herself must run in order to make her body strong. (See E. S. Curtis, vol. 1, pp. 46–47, 124–25.)

Page 39 / Translated from the Paviotso, in E. S. Curtis, vol. 15, p. 79. Recited at the close of the girls' puberty ceremony, while the girl is being ritually bathed in a stream or spring.

Page 40 / Translated from the Zuni by Ruth Bunzel, in her "Zuñi Ritual Poetry," pp. 797–98. A boy who has been cured of a serious illness by the members of a medicine society may later be initiated into the society in order to protect himself against any recurrence of the disease. The initiation takes place during a full moon.

Page 41 / Translated from the Zuni by Ruth Bunzel, in her "Zuñi Ritual Poetry," p. 808. *Dawn Lake:* "The water that lies on the easternmost rim of the world. This is where the sun comes out, and stands, therefore, as a symbol of fulfillment" ("Zuñi Ritual Poetry," p. 625).

Page 42 / Translated from the Chippewa by Frances Densmore, in her *Chippewa Music,* pp. 30–41. A few of the many songs sung over a period of several days. The Midéwiwin (muh-DAY-wuh-win), or Medicine Society, is a secret religious organization, formerly influential among the Chippewa. Its purpose is to lengthen the lives of its members, which it attempts to do by means of herbs, singing, and magic rituals. *In the center:* translation follows Thomas Vennum, Jr., "Ojibwa Origin-Migration Songs of the *Mitewiwin,*" *Journal of American Folklore,* vol. 91 (1978), p. 773. *Bubbling spring:* an imagined wellspring carrying the *migis,* or sacred cowrie shell, used in healing rituals of the Midéwiwin.

Love Songs and Love Magic

Page 47 / Translated from the Eskimo by Paul-Emile Victor, p. 24.

Page 48 / My translation of the Aztec text in Ruiz, pp. 109–10. One of more than fifty magic spells collected in rural areas south of Mexico City during the early 1600s by the Catholic priest Hernando Ruiz de Alarcón. *Xochiquetzal* (show-chee-KET-sahl): the goddess of love. *With a snake at her hips, around her loins:* follows the Aztec text in Michael D. Coe and Gordon Whittaker, *Aztec Sorcerers in Seventeenth Century Mexico: The Treatise on Superstitions by Hernando Ruiz de Alcarcón,* Institute for Mesoamerican Studies, State University of New York at Albany, 1982, p. 189. *The young warrior:* the sun. *Risen . . . Born:* a play on words (both verbs can refer either to sunrise or to childbirth). The idea seems to be that the speaker will be able to attract a woman because he was born from a woman.

Page 49 / Translated from the Quechua by R. and M. d'Harcourt, p. 484 (the English version is mine, after the French of the d'Harcourts).

Page 50 / Translated from the lingua geral by J. Vieira Couto de Magalhães, vol. 2, pp. 140–41 (the English version is mine, after the Portuguese of Magalhães). Rudá was the god of love, imagined as a warrior who lived in the clouds. His function was to arouse longing in the hearts of hunters and warriors, causing them to shorten their journeys and turn their steps toward home. As she chants this prayer, the woman extends her arms in the direction she believes her loved one to be. *Make it be that he:* The user substitutes the name of her lover for the pronoun.

Page 51 / Interpreted from Chippewa pictographs by H. R. Schoolcraft, vol. 1, pp. 403–4 and pl. 56, fig. A. Although the Chippewa had no writing in the modern sense, they preserved many of their songs in picture symbols, or pictographs, drawn on birch bark. Each of the six lines in this love song is represented by a single picture.

Page 52 / Translated from the Arekuna by Cesáreo de Armellada, p. 246 (the English version is mine, after the Spanish of Armellada). A magic spell, or *tarén,* to be used by a man who is lovesick. See note to p. 14, above.

Page 53 / Translated from the Cherokee by J. F. and A. G. Kilpatrick, in their *Walk in Your Soul,* p. 116. The speaker, who may be of either sex, first says or thinks the name of the loved one, then recites the spell four times. *Red:* stands for victory, or power. *You are a Wizard!:* The line is either self-directed, as the Kilpatricks suggest, or directed to an unknown spirit helper.

Page 54 / Translated from the Cherokee by J. F. and A. G. Kilpatrick, in their *Run Toward the Nightland,* p. 64. Used by a man for putting to sleep a desired woman (and her entire family as well). He says it four times, and after each time blows his breath toward the woman's house.

Page 55 / Translated from the Quechua by Garcilaso de la Vega (the English version is mine, after the Spanish of Garcilaso as reproduced in Lara, p. 45). This famous little song, believed to have been used by the Incas before the Spanish Conquest, has generally been mistranslated as: "To my song / You will sleep. / At midnight / I will come."

Page 56 / Translated from the Quechua by J. M. Arguedas, p. 17 (the English version is mine, after the Spanish of Arguedas). According to Arguedas, this is a song for dancing the *huayño,* a couple dance believed to be of pre-Columbian origin and still popular in the highlands of southern Peru. Although the melodies strike the non-Indian ear as plaintive and the typically erotic lyrics are often mournful, occasionally sinister, the *huayño* as defined by Arguedas is in fact a pleasure dance. The term "ginger ale bottle," appearing in the Quechua text as *chinchir botellapsis* is a reminder that North American-style soft drinks are well known in the Andes, even in remote Indian villages.

Page 58 / Translated from the Kwakiutl by Franz Boas, in his "Songs," pp. 5–6. Among the Kwakiutl, love songs and mourning songs are designated by a single term. Love songs are sung in a manner that imitates crying, high-pitched and quavering. In the old days a crowd of boys would march up and down the street of the village singing such songs to taunt the girls. (See Boas, *Kwakiutl Ethnography,* p. 348.)

Page 59 / Translated from the Chippewa by Frances Densmore, in her *Chippewa Music,* pp. 150–51. Chippewa love songs have unusually attractive melodies of a mournful character, sung with a reedy, nasal tone that imitates the Chippewa flute.

Page 60 / Translated from the Quechua by J. M. Arguedas, p. 26 (the English version is mine, after the Spanish of Arguedas). Another *huayño* (see note to p. 56, above). *Llámran:* a tree similar to the alder (Jesús Lara, *Diccionario Qhëshwa-Castellano Castellano-Qhëshwa*). *Tara:* a kind of tree.

Page 61 / Translated from the Quechua by Lucinda Hart-González, p. 2. Yet another *huayño* (see notes to pp. 56 and 60, above).

For the Traveler

Page 65 / Translated from the Flathead by A. P. Merriam, p. 5. The native informant, Madeline Charley, explained that this song "expresses a joy of living." In performance, the words are spoken in a normal voice, preceded by these meaningless syllables sung in clear, lilting tones: *hey-ya-ah, hey-ya-yuh, hey-ya-ii, hey-ya-a-a-ii, ay-ya-ii.* After the spoken section, the song concludes with another group of lilting syllables, fading to a whisper: *hey-ya-ii, hey-ya-yuh-ii, aii, yo-oh.*

Page 66 / Translated from the Maya by Carl Sapper, pp. 289–90 (the English version is mine, after the German of Sapper). *Copal:* resin of the copal tree, used as incense in religious ceremonies. *Your food, your drink:* the copal. *Trogon:* a medium-sized woodland bird.

Page 68 / My translation of the Aztec text in Ruiz, p. 68. This and several related spells, perhaps all belonging to a single ritual, were found written on a piece of paper lying in the road near a river. They form part of the large collection of Aztec incantations assembled in 1629 by Ruiz de Alarcón, who was able to learn that this particular spell was used by porters who carried heavy loads from town to town. See note to p. 48, above.

Page 69 / Translated from the Cherokee by J. F. and A. G. Kilpatrick, in their *Run Toward the Nightland,* p. 47. To be spoken only once after the beginning of a journey. It is said that if the traveler turns back after reciting the spell, he will suffer unnatural fatigue. *Leech:* a wormlike animal remarkable for its ability to lengthen or shorten its body. *Hummingbird:* noted for quickness. *Dayi!:* a word like "whoosh" or "zoom," suggesting speed.

Page 70 / Translated from the Zuni by F. H. Cushing, p. 42 (the version given here is mine, based on Cushing's Zuni text and interlinear translation, using the phraseology developed by Ruth Bunzel). Addressed to the prey gods of the war cult, here represented by the traveler's fetish, a small stone carved in the shape of a beast of prey. *Prayer meal:* cornmeal sprinkled as an offering. *Divine ones:* literally, "raw beings," a term applied to nonhuman entities (humans are "cooked beings"). *Mountain Lion! . . . Knife Wing!:* names of two of the prey gods.

Page 72 / Translated from the Papago by Ruth Underhill and revised by D. M. Bahr et al., in Underhill et al., pp. 54–55. Each year Papago men make an arduous journey across the desert in order to bring back salt from the ocean. Along the way they hope to have a vision in which a guardian spirit (here called the "made father") will give them the strength to endure hardship. The speech itself is a form of magic, describing the ideal salt pilgrimage, addressed to the younger men so they will be sure to have the vision that is expected of them. *Acts this way:* A salt pilgrim must not be softened by thoughts of home. *My days were completed:* the four days' preparation before the journey begins. *West lying road:* toward the ocean. *Hungerness:* the ability to endure hunger. *Four times spilled the coming dawn:* of the four preparatory days (?).

Page 74 / Translated from the Sioux by Frances Densmore, in her *Teton Sioux Music,* pp. 299–300. The Horse Society was one of several "dream societies" among the Sioux, each composed of men who had dreamed of the same animal. Horse songs, received in dreams, were used in meetings and on the warpath to make the horse swift and sure.

Page 75 / Translated from the Navajo, in Hill, "Navaho Trading," p. 384. The song is repeated six times with minor variations. In the first repetition the phrase "is starting toward me" changes to "is coming toward me." In the second repetition it changes to "has come to me"; in the third, "has become mine"; in the fourth, "walks about me," and so forth. Sung while traveling to trade with a distant tribe, the song helps the traveler imagine the beautiful horse and other goods that may come his way as the result of a profitable trade. It is believed that songs of this type help to ensure successful bargaining.

Against Sickness and Evil

Page 79 / Translated from the Uitoto by K. T. Preuss, in his *Religion,* p. 631 (the English version is mine, after the Uitoto text and interlinear

German translation given by Preuss). *Father Kumu:* an ancestor spirit responsible for headaches. *Drunk:* by means of tobacco. *Don't be my child:* Father Kumu sends pain in the form of an image of himself (a "phantom man"), which the sufferer regards as his own, unwelcome child. *Sweet herb:* an unidentified herb that drives away sickness.

Page 80 / My translation of the Aztec text in Ruiz, p. 152. Magic spells like this one were in common use among Aztec healers of the early 1600s, many if not most of whom were women.

Page 81 / Collected in 1960 by William R. Holland in the township of Larrainzar, Chiapas, Mexico; translated from the Maya into Spanish by Pascual Hernández T'ul, in Sodi, p. 85 (the English version is mine, after the Spanish of Hernández T'ul). *Caused by a dream:* caused by the separation of soul and body during a dream (see W. R. Holland and R. G. Tharp, "Highland Maya Psychotherapy," *American Antropologist,* vol. 66, p. 44). *Pulse:* Tzotzil curers place great significance in the pulse, which they frequently test by feeling the patient's wrist.

Page 82 / Translated from the Navajo by Gladys Reichard, p. 31. The Shooting Chant is one of the nine-day healing ceremonials of the Navajo. *Given the wink:* warned by a wink to say nothing.

Page 83 / My translation of the Aztec text in Sahagún, bk. 1, ch. 12. Addressed to the god Tezcatlipoca. When the sinner has finished his prayer, he lists his sins, and the sorcerer prescribes a fitting punishment, such as fasting or bloodletting. *Common man:* a manner of speaking used in prayer; in fact, the sinner may be a nobleman.

Page 84 / Translated from the Kwakiutl by Franz Boas, in his *Religion of the Kwakiutl Indians,* pt. 2, p. 184.

Page 85 / Translated from the Eskimo by Knud Rasmussen, in his *Netsilik Eskimos,* pp. 284–85 (translated from Rasmussen's Danish into English by W. E. Calvert). Magic words such as these, either spoken or chanted, are calculated to impart vitality. The words are private property, passed from father to son, and must not be uttered where others can overhear.

Page 86 / Translated from the Navajo by Johnny C. Cooke and K. W. Luckert, in Luckert, p. 86. Coyoteway is one of the nine-day healing ceremonials of the Navajo, performed by a chanter for the benefit of at least several participants, including a principal beneficiary, called the "patient." As the chanter sings the "sprinkling song" given here, he throws medicine on each of the participants, whose bodies become mystically united with the body of Coyote. *The Furs are put in the water:* The participants' bodies (as though their skins, or "furs," were Coyote's) are doused with the medicinal water.

Page 87 / Translated from the Modoc, in Kroeber, *Handbook,* p. 321. Entirely unexplained, these mystical healing songs seemingly refer to the dreams, or visions, of the medicine man as his soul takes leave of his body, seeks spiritual power in a distant world, and returns to earth with a song that will help cure his patient. Such, in any event, is a classic pattern in the art of the shaman, or medicine man. *I, the song:* probably means "I, the spirit," where the song given by the spirit and the spirit itself are so closely connected that a single word indicates either one (see Leslie Spier, *Klamath Ethnography,* University of California Publications in American Archaeology and Ethnology, vol. 30, 1930, p. 239.

Page 88 / Translated from the Blackfeet by G. B. Grinnell, p. 285. The patient, in the last stages of tuberculosis, lay stripped to the waist as the medicine man, kneeling before him, burned a pinch of sweet grass over live coals. After rubbing himself with the smoke, he began tapping rapidly on a drum, reciting this prayer. Afterward he dipped an eagle feather into a cup of clear liquid and applied it to the patient's chest. *Listen, my dream!:* Each medicine man has his "dream, or secret helper, to whom he prays for aid" (Grinnell's note).

Page 89 / Translated from the Mazatec by Alvaro Estrada, p. 208 (translated from Estrada's Spanish into English by Henry Munn). Under the influence of narcotic mushrooms, Mazatec healers make imaginary journeys to distant places in order to acquire spiritual power or to guide home the "lost" soul of the sick person. *Thirteen:* may be freely translated as "a magic number of" or "a wonderful quantity of"; the number thirteen is used automatically in both Mazatec and Mayan chants (compare the Tzotzil Maya prayer on p. 81, above). *Big clown:*

perhaps a reference to God, imagined as good-humored and exuberant (compare Estrada, pp. 218–20).

Page 90 / Translated from the Sioux by Frances Densmore, in her *Teton Sioux Music,* pp. 249 and 250.

Page 91 / Translated from the Mbyá by León Cadogan, p. 24 (the English version is mine, after the Spanish of Cadogan). These words, recited at dawn, are said to be part of the daily routine of every orthodox Mbyá. *Spirit Father:* Ñamandu ("Spirit Father"), the Creator. *Great-Heart Spirit:* the sun.

Controlling the Weather

Page 95 / Translated from the Eskimo by H. H. Roberts and D. Jenness, pp. 334, 492 (the version given here, based on the lexical translation of Roberts and Jenness, is by C. M. Bowra, from his *Primitive Song,* 1962, p. 62). *Man outside:* the singer's guardian spirit. Note: The original performance of this song is included in the album *A Cry from the Earth,* Folkways Records, 1979, FC 7777.

Page 96 / Translated from the Arekuna by Cesáreo de Armellada, p. 87 (the English version is mine, after the Spanish of Armellada). A magic spell, or *tarén,* to turn back a rainstorm, See note to p. 14, above.

Page 97 / Translated from the Cherokee by James Mooney, p. 387. A magic spell for driving away a storm that threatens to injure the growing corn. Mooney writes: "The first part is a meaningless song, which is sung in a low tone. . . . The storm, which is not directly named, is then addressed and declared to be coming on in a fearful manner on the track of his wife, like an animal in the rutting season. The shaman points out her tracks directed toward the upper regions and begs the storm to follow her along the waving treetops of the lofty mountains, where he shall be undisturbed."

Page 98 / Translated from the Blackfeet, in E. S. Curtis, vol. 18, p. 185. A fictional prayer from a myth in which three girls caught in a thunderstorm take refuge under a tree. The eldest delivers the prayer and is later obliged to make good on her promise.

Page 99 / Translated from the Haida by J. R. Swanton, p. 16.

Page 100 / Translated from the Kwakiutl, in E. S. Curtis, vol. 10, p. 63. Addressed to an overhanging cliff. When the cliff has been passed, the boatman turns his head and says, "Thank you, Old Man, that we have passed safely."

Page 101 / Translated from the Yahgan by Martin Gusinde, p. 1057 (the English version is mine, after the German of Gusinde). One of several dozen short, deceptively simple Yahgan prayers collected by Gusinde, who reported that the words were handed down unchanged from generation to generation. *Father:* The Supreme Being.

Page 102 / Translated from the Nootka, in Densmore, *Nootka and Quileute Music,* p. 284.

Page 103 / Translated from the Eskimo by E. S. Carpenter, in his *Anerca.*

Page 104 / Translated from the Kwakiutl by Franz Boas, in his *Religion of the Kwakiutl Indians,* pt. 2, p. 190.

Page 105 / Translated from the Navajo by Washington Matthews, p. 459. Thunder songs, calling for rain, are used in Navajo healing ceremonials in order to secure the blessings that rain symbolizes. The nearly identical paired stanzas are characteristic of many Southwest Indian songs. *Thonah!:* the sound of thunder.

Page 106 / Translated from the Zuni by Ruth Bunzel, in her "Zuñi Ritual Poetry, pp. 640–41. At midwinter no one is allowed to take out ashes for a period of ten days. As the fires continue to burn inside the houses, it is as though the houses were filling up with corn, symbolized by the growing piles of ashes. At the end of the ten days, the prohibition is lifted, and the official Fire Keeper delivers this "special request." *A fourfold robe of white meal:* snow. *Our mothers:* A cob of seed corn is a "mother." *They will stretch out their hands:* The new corn plants will extend their

170

leaves. *With our thoughts following them:* devoting our thoughts to the corn (in a well-known Zuni myth the corn spirits, feeling they were no longer appreciated, disappeared).

Planting and Gathering

Page 111 / Translated from the Cágaba by K. T. Preuss, in his "Forschungreise," vol. 20 (1925), p. 84 (the version given here, after the German of Preuss, is by Paul Radin, from his *Monotheism Among Primitive Peoples,* Special Publications of the Bollingen Foundation, no. 4, p. 15).

Page 112 / Translated from the Maya by J. E. S. Thompson, p. 45 (the version given here is mine, based on Thompson's interlinear translation). The evening before the little field, or milpa, is to be cleared, friends of the man whose garden it will be gather at his home for an all-night vigil. At dawn the man sets out for the forest, followed at some distance by fifteen to twenty-five of his friends, who will help with the felling. Upon reaching the chosen spot, the owner, alone, burns a lump of incense and recites this prayer.

Page 113 / Translated from the Arikara, in E. S. Curtis, vol. 5, p. 72. In early spring, before the planting season, the Arikara held a ritual to promote the growth of crops. Men carried war weapons, and women hoes, in a dance believed to have the double effect of preparing the earth for planting and protecting the garden from enemies. Following this, a priest with eyes fixed on a Sioux scalp chanted the prayer given here (in a style described as "throwing out a short passage with breathless rapidity and extreme vehemence, to be followed by a few words in more measured time").

Page 114 / Translated from the Papago by Ruth Underhill, in her *Papago Indian Religion,* p. 147. Sung to the accompaniment of scraping sticks and basket drums during the midwinter *wíikita,* or prayer stick festival.

Page 115 / Translated from the Seneca by J. N. B. Hewitt, in Curtin and Hewitt, p. 651. From a myth of the origin of the Corn Dance. The songs are said to have been taught in the ancient days by the corn spirits themselves, so that people could express thanks when the corn ripens.

Page 116 / My translation of the Aztec text in Ruiz, p. 88. *My uncles, the spirits:* the animals who have been destroying the corn. *My father,* 4 Reed: the fire (Aztec deities are often addressed by calendrical names such as 4 Reed, actually a date, like Tuesday the third or the tenth of May).

Page 117 / Translated from the Maya by Carl Sapper, pp. 293–94 (the English version is mine, after the German of Sapper). The prayer is made three days before the corn harvest, at home in the evening with a burnt offering of resin, or copal, in front of a Christian cross.

Page 118 / Translated from the Tewa by H. J. Spinden, p. 106. According to myth, the corn mothers were the first mothers of the Tewa people. From them each child receives his soul at birth. In ritual they are represented by ears of corn. (See Ortiz, pp. 13, 32.)

Page 119 / Translated from the Arapaho by A. L. Kroeber, in his *Arapaho,* p. 314. *Our father:* the Supreme Being. *Our grandfather:* probably the sun (compare the prayer on p. 32). *All those that shine:* the stars.

Page 120 / Translated from the Modoc by V. F. Ray, p. 28. The first half of this prayer is addressed to the earth (with an offering of food), the second half to the sun. *Camas:* a lily with edible bulbs, formerly a staple food.

Page 121 / Translated from the Havasupai by Leslie Spier, p. 286. In praying to the sun, a Havasupai would draw his hands down over his face, blowing to brush away evil.

For the Hunter

Page 125 / Translated from the Zuni by Ruth Bunzel, in her "Zuñi Katcinas," p. 1043 (the translation given here has been slightly revised, following E. C. Parsons, *Pueblo Indian Religion,* University of Chicago

Press, 1939, p. 302). An offering of wafer bread (a kind of tortilla) is thrown into the fire. The ghosts, it is believed, will absorb the odor.

Page 126 / Translated from the Pawnee by Gene Weltfish, p. 6. Recalls the moment when the hunter early in the morning sights a buffalo standing quietly, waiting for sunrise.

Page 127 / Translated from the Sioux by Frances Densmore, in her *Teton Sioux Music*, p. 288. Songs of this type are said to have been received in dreams about buffalo. In the Buffalo Dance itself, it was customary for the dancers to wear headdresses decorated with buffalo horns and to imitate the actions of buffalo.

Page 128 / Translated from the Omaha by Francis La Flesche, p. 633.

Page 129 / Translated from the Kwakiutl by Franz Boas, in his *Religion of the Kwakiutl Indians,* pt. 2, pp. 193–94. The Kwakiutl supplicant stands or sits before the one he is praying to and fixes his eyes upon it (Boas, *Kwakiutl Ethnography,* p. 156).

Page 130 / Translated from the Eskimo by Knud Rasmussen, in his *Iglulik Eskimos,* pp. 167–68 (translated from Rasmussen's Danish into English by W. Worster).

Page 131 / Translated from the Nootka, in E. S. Curtis, vol. 11, p. 37. While praying, the whaler squats on a rock in the water and rubs his hands.

Page 132 / Translated from the Eskimo by William Thalbitzer, p. 258. This spell was used to subdue the fierceness of the animal when it had been harpooned and the close fighting began. Obtained from an informant named Akernilik. "But it was of no use to me," added Akernilik. "I never succeeded in getting a walrus."

Page 133 / Translated from the Papago by Ruth Underhill, in her *Papago Indian Religion,* p. 251. One of a series of songs dreamed by an eagle hunter.

Page 134 / Translated from the Yokuts by A. L. Kroeber, in his *Hand-*

book, p. 529. The eagle is captured in a noose rigged to a stuffed animal skin used as bait. Afterward, the hunter kills the eagle by stepping on it.

Page 135 / Translated from the Papago by Ruth Underhill and revised by D. M. Bahr et al., in Underhill et al., pp. 79–80. This mysterious spell may be explained by comparing it with the similar Navajo prayer immediately following. *They rubbed themselves with [the tail of the deer]:* When a deer has been killed, the tail is cut off and each man rubs his body with it as a blessing (Underhill, *Papago Indian Religion,* p. 102).

Page 136 / Translated from the Navajo by W. W. Hill, in his *Agricultural and Hunting Methods,* pp. 128–29. When the hunting party was ready to return, after a number of killed deer had been defleshed and the meat dried and stored in buckskin sacks, then the bones and horns were laid out on a bed of boughs in a prescribed order from north to south. If the first deer killed had been a buck, a turquoise bead was placed between its horns (if a doe, a white-shell bead was put on its head), and the prayer given here was recited. *That we may continue to hold each other with the turquoise hand:* I take this to mean "that we may continue to hold each other by the hand in a precious, or turquoise-like, manner." In the case of a doe, the term would be "white-shell hand." *Beautifully:* I have changed Hill's "pleasantly" to "beautifully"; the Navajo term is *hozhogo,* variously rendered by Navajo specialists as "pleasantly," "nicely," "happily," "beautifully."

Page 138 / Translated from the Zuni by F. H. Cushing, pp. 33–34 (the version given here is mine, based on Cushing's Zuni text and interlinear translation, using the phraseology developed by Ruth Bunzel). Deer and other game are believed to be under the influence of those animals that naturally prey upon them. The heart of the deer at all times "obeys" the heart of the predator, whose breath, regarded as an exhalation from the heart, can overcome the deer even at great distances. The power of the predators is systematized in a pantheon of six prey gods, called "beast priests," and, in a sense, is symbolized by ferocious, outsize prototypes that in mythic times were shriveled by lightning and burned into stone. These stones, in which the heart of the beast still lives, are kept as fetishes and must be carried while hunting. The fetish, it is believed, will intercede with the "beast priests," enabling the hunter to make a kill. The prayer given here is from the great hunt held at the winter solstice. *My father, my mother:* addressing the fetish. *Unexpectedly . . . with whatever:* I take this to be an apology for any mistake or insufficiency connected with the offering. *I have passed you on your road:* I meet you. *Dance priests:* gods of the sacred dances, another name for the "beast priests," or prey gods. *Plume wands:* prayer sticks, which the spirit of the fetish will convey to the prey gods. *Prayer meal:* a mixture of cornmeal and precious additives (such as turquoise dust). *Light:* The word for light, *tekohanane* (literally, "white-space"), is also the word for life.

For the Dying and the Dead

Page 143 / Translated from the Tlingit by Frederica de Laguna, pp. 1313–14. Only the first stanza of a two-stanza song is given here. The song is typical of the many mourning songs and songs about dying that are performed at potlatch ceremonies, one purpose of which is to honor the dead.

Page 144 / Translated from the Tsimshian by Marius Barbeau, p. 132 (the version given here is mine, based on Barbeau's lexical translation). Another potlatch song (see note to p. 143, above).

Page 145 / Translated from the Quechua by J. M. Arguedas, p. 46 (the English version is mine, after the Spanish of Arguedas). This song comes from the rural province of Paucartambo (near Cuzco) on the eastern edge of the Andes, at the beginning of the jungle—the "great forest"— that stretches away toward Brazil. Family and friends gather to watch over the corpse the night before the burial. At three in the morning they proceed to the cemetery and sing this song at the cemetery gate (Arguedas, p. 13). *Coca:* the source of cocaine; its leaf is chewed as a narcotic. *Dove:* loved one. *Little bell:* perhaps refers to a church bell in the town of Paucartambo, capital of the province.

Page 146 / Translated from the Crow by R. H. Lowie, pp. 441–42. The typical Crow prayer was for long life. Yet there were exceptional individuals, especially young warriors, who deliberately courted death. Such men were called "crazy-dogs-wishing-to-die." For them the war

fervor always present in any Crow camp had become a summons to
self-sacrifice. In the crazy-dog prayer quoted here—actually an excerpt
from a somewhat longer prayer—we have reached, as Robert Lowie believed, "the peak of the Crow spirit" (Lowie, *The Crow Indians,* Holt,
Rinehart and Winston, 1935, pp. 332–34). *You Above:* probably the sun.
Inside the Earth: regarded by Lowie as a "nonce-god," a momentary in-
spiration not sanctified by Crow dogma.

Page 147 / Translated from the Kiowa, in Rhodes, *Kiowa,* p. 18. Mem-
bership in the Kiowa Crazy-Dog Society was limited to the ten bravest
warriors in the tribe. The song given here was sung in 1871 by the famous Kiowa warrior Setanke, after he had been arrested for participat-
ing in a raid on a wagon train—and immediately before making a suici-
dal assault on his white guard.

Page 148 / My translation from the Aztec, in Bierhorst, *Cantares Mexicanos,* song 89, stanzas 7–8. A fictional lament from a song-ritual in
which an imaginary battle is staged. *Goes song-weeping:* a figurative expression meaning "goes to war." *Ocotepec:* an Aztec town. *Gorge:* the bat-
tlefield, figuratively speaking. *Crimson:* the red land of the sunrise, where
the souls of dead warriors go. *The Shore:* the sunrise land, the hereafter.
Bereavement flowers: songs of lamentation. *I seek you:* I seek to bring your
ghost back to earth by means of these songs.

Page 149 / Translated from the Wintu by Dorothy Demetracopoulou
(i.e., Dorothy Demetracopoulou Lee), p. 487. A song of the Wintu
Dream Dance cult, which appears to have been related to the Ghost
Dance movement that swept through the West during the last quarter
of the nineteenth century. Wintu Dream songs were given to men and
women in their sleep by the ghost of a dead relative or friend. In the
morning the dreamer sang the song and danced to it.

Page 150 / Translated from the Omaha by R. F. Fortune, p. 78. Heard
in a nightmare by an Omaha woman who exorcised the ghosts the next
morning by throwing bread to the four winds. Ghosts as whirlwinds or
in human form walking on the air a foot or two above the ground were
well known to all members of the Omaha tribe (Fortune, p. 81).

Page 151 / Translated from the Winnebago by Paul Radin, pp. 141–42. In the evening, after the corpse has been buried, the mourners gather indoors for a solemn feast. A speaker greets the assembled guests, lights a pipe, and, passing a bit of tobacco behind him through an opening in the lodge, recites this prayer.

Page 152 / My translation of the Aztec text in Sahagún, bk, 3, app. 1, pp. 39–40. Spoken as the corpse lay stretched out before an audience of mourners. Afterward the body was cremated and the ashes buried either at home or at a family shrine.

Page 153 / Translated from the Tewa by Alfonso Ortiz, p. 54. The soul is believed to haunt the village for four days following death. On the fourth night, relatives gather to perform a "releasing" rite in which the ghost is offered food mingled with tobacco smoke at an outdoor shrine some distance from the house. On the way back the party stops four times, and each person, at each stop, faces the shrine, spits out a bit of charcoal, and draws four lines in the earth. Back at the house, the lead elder softly recites the prayer given here. *Muddied:* by means of the tobacco smoke. *Shadows:* caused by the charcoal. *Gullies:* the lines. *Ask for these things:* intercede with other spirits in our behalf.

Page 154 / Translated from the Omaha by R. F. Fortune, p. 49. Recited in order to drive away the ghost, which is thought to be carried by the wind.

Arguedas, José María. *Canciones y cuentos del pueblo quechua.* Lima: Editorial Huascarán, 1949.

Armellada, Cesáreo de. *Pemontón taremurú: Invocaciones mágicas de los indios pemón.* Caracas: Universidad Católica Andrés Bello, 1972.

Barbeau, Marius. "Tsimshian Songs." In Viola E. Garfield, Paul S. Wingert, and Marius Barbeau, *The Tsimshian: Their Arts and Music.* Publications of the American Ethnological Society, XVIII, 1951.

Bierhorst, John. *Cantares Mexicanos: Songs of the Aztecs.* Stanford: Stanford University Press, forthcoming.

Boas, Franz. *Kwakiutl Ethnography.* Edited by Helen Codere. Chicago: University of Chicago Press, 1966.

―――. "Songs of the Kwakiutl Indians." *Internationales Archiv für Ethnographie,* vol. 9, supplement, pp. 1–9 Leiden, 1896.

―――. *The Religion of the Kwakiutl Indians.* Columbia University Contributions to Anthropology, vol. 10. New York: Columbia University Press, 1930.

Bunzel, Ruth. "Zuñi Katcinas." *Forty-seventh Annual Report of the Bureau of American Ethnology, 1929-30,* pp. 837–1086. Washington, 1932.

―――. "Zuñi Ritual Poetry." *Forty-seventh Annual Report of the Bureau of American Ethnology, 1929-30,* pp. 611–835. Washington, 1932.

Cadogan, León. *Ayvu Rapyta: Textos míticos de los Mbyá-Guaraní del Guairá.* Universidade de São Paulo, Faculdade de Filosofia, Ciências e Letras, Boletim 227, Antropologia 5. São Paulo, 1959.

Carpenter, Edmund, *Anerca*. Toronto: J. M. Dent & Sons, 1959.

Curtin, Jeremiah, and Hewitt, J. N. B. "Seneca Fiction, Legends, and Myths." *Thirty-second Annual Report of the Bureau of American Ethnology, 1910–11*, pp. 37–819. Washington, 1918.

Curtis, Edward S. *The North American Indian*, 20 vols. Vols. 1–5: Cambridge, Mass.; vols. 6–20: Norwood, Mass.; 1907–30.

Curtis, Natalie. *The Indians' Book*. New York: Dover, 1968.

Cushing, Frank Hamilton. "Zuñi Fetiches." *Second Annual Report of the Bureau of American Ethnology, 1880–81*, pp. 3–45. Washington, 1883.

de Laguna, Frederica. *Under Mount Saint Elias: The History and Culture of the Yakutat Tlingit*. 3 parts. Smithsonian Contributions to Anthropology, vol. 7 (1972).

d'Harcourt, R., and d'Harcourt, M. *La musique des Incas et ses survivances*. Paris: Librairie Orientaliste Paul Geuthner, 1925.

Demetracopoulou, D[orothy]. "Wintu Songs," *Anthropos*, vol. 30 (1935), pp. 483–94.

Densmore, Frances. *Chippewa Music*. Bureau of American Ethnology Bulletin 45. Washington, 1910.

————. *Nootka and Quileute Music*. Bureau of American Ethnology Bulletin 124. Washington, 1939.

————. *Teton Sioux Music*. Bureau of American Ethnology Bulletin 61. Washington, 1918.

Estrada, Alvaro. *María Sabina: Her Life and Chants*. Translated from the Spanish, with commentaries, by Henry Munn; retrospective essay by R. Gordon Wasson; preface by Jerome Rothenberg. Santa Barbara: Ross-Erikson, 1981.

Farrer, Claire R. "Singing for Life: The Mescalero Apache Girls' Puberty Ceremony." In Charlotte J. Frisbie, ed., *Southwestern Indian Ritual Drama*. Albuquerque: School of American Research and University of New Mexico Press, 1980.

Fortune, R. F. *Omaha Secret Societies*. Columbia University Contributions to Anthropology, vol. 14. New York: Columbia University Press, 1932.

Goddard, Pliny Earle. *Jicarilla Apache Texts*. Anthropological Papers of the American Museum of Natural History, vol. 8. New York, 1911.

———. "The Masked Dancers of the Apache." *Holmes Anniversary Volume,* pp. 132–36. Washington, 1916.

Grinnell, George Bird. *Blackfoot Lodge Tales: The Story of a Prairie People*. Lincoln: University of Nebraska Press, 1962. Originally published in 1892.

Gusinde, Martin. *Die Feuerland Indianer,* vol. 2: "Die Yamana." Mödling bei Wien: Anthropos, 1937.

Hart-González, Lucinda. "Language Change in Quechua Verse." *Latin American Indian Literatures*. Latin American Monograph Series, no. 11, pp. 1–11. Northwestern Pennsylvania Institute for Latin American Studies, Mercyhurst College. Erie, 1980.

Hill, W. W. "Navaho Trading and Trading Ritual: A Study of Cultural Dynamics." *Southwestern Journal of Anthropology,* vol. 4 (1948), pp. 371–96.

———. *The Agricultural and Hunting Methods of the Navaho Indians.* Yale University Publications in Anthropology, no. 18. New Haven, 1938.

Kilpatrick, Jack Frederick, and Kilpatrick, Anna Gritts. *Run Toward the Nightland: Magic of the Oklahoma Cherokees.* Dallas: Southern Methodist University Press, 1967.

————. *Walk in Your Soul: Love Incantations of the Oklahoma Cherokees.* Dallas: Southern Methodist University Press, 1965.

Kroeber, Alfred L. *Handbook of the Indians of California.* Bureau of American Ethnology Bulletin 78. Washington, 1925.

————. *The Arapaho.* Bulletin of the American Museum of Natural History, vol. 18. New York, 1902.

La Flesche, Francis. "The Osage Tribe: Rite of the Wa-xo´-be." *Forty-fifth Annual Report of the Bureau of American Ethnology, 1927–28,* pp. 523–833. Washington, 1930.

Lara, Jesús. *La literatura de los quechuas.* 2d ed. La Paz, Bolivia: Librería y Editorial Juventud, 1969.

Lowie, Robert H. "Crow Prayers." *American Anthropologist,* vol. 35 (1933), pp. 433–42.

Luckert, Karl W. *Coyoteway: A Navajo Holyway Healing Ceremonial.* Tucson and Flagstaff: University of Arizona Press and Museum of Northern Arizona Press, 1979.

Magalhães, [J. Vieira] Couto de. *O Selvagem.* 2 vols. in one. Rio de Janeiro: Typographia da Reforma, 1876.

Matthews, Washington. "The Mountain Chant: A Navajo Ceremony." *Fifth Annual Report of the Bureau of American Ethnology, 1883–84,* pp. 379–467. Washington, 1887.

Merriam, Alan P. "Songs and Dances of the Flathead Indians." Folkways album FE 4445 (phonograph disc with booklet). New York: Folkways Records, 1953.

Mooney, James. "The Sacred Formulas of the Cherokees." *Seventh Annual Report of the Bureau of American Ethnology, 1885–86,* pp. 301–97. Washington, 1891.

Neihardt, John G. *Black Elk Speaks: Being the Life Story of a Holy Man of the Oglala Sioux*. Lincoln: University of Nebraska Press, 1961.

Ortiz, Alfonso. *The Tewa World: Space, Time, Being, and Becoming in a Pueblo Society*. Chicago: University of Chicago Press, 1969.

Preuss, Konrad Theodor. "Forschungreise zu den Kágaba-Indianern der Sierra Nevada de Santa Marta in Kolumbien." *Anthropos*, vols. 14–22 (1919–27).

———. *Religion und Mythologie der Uitoto*. Göttingen: Vandenhoeck & Ruprecht, 1921–23.

Radin, Paul. "The Winnebago Tribe." *Thirty-seventh Annual Report of the Bureau of American Ethnology, 1915–16*, pp. 35–550. Washington, 1923.

Rasmussen, Knud. *Intellectual Culture of the Iglulik Eskimos*. Report of the Fifth Thule Expedition 1921–24, vol. 7, no. 1. Translated from the Danish by W. Worster. Copenhagen: Gyldendalske Boghandel, 1929.

———. *The Netsilik Eskimos: Social Life and Spiritual Culture*. Report of the Fifth Thule Expedition 1921–24, vol, 8, nos. 1–2. Translated from the Danish by W. E. Calvert. Copenhagen: Gyldendalske Boghandel, 1931.

Ray, Verne F. *Primitive Pragmatists: The Modoc Indians of Northern California*. Seattle: University of Washington Press, 1963.

Reichard, Gladys A. *Prayer: The Compulsive Word*. Seattle: University of Washington Press, 1944.

Rhodes, Willard. "Indian Songs of Today." Unpaged typescript to be published as a booklet accompanying Library of Congress phonograph album AFS-L36: "Indian Songs of Today." Library of Congress, Archive of Folk Song.

————. "Music of the American Indian: Kiowa." Booklet accompanying Library of Congress phonograph album AFS-L35. Library of Congress, Archive of Folk Song, no date.

Roberts, Helen H., and Jenness, Diamond. *Songs of the Copper Eskimo.* Report of the Canadian Arctic Expedition 1913–18, vol. 14. Ottawa, 1925.,

Ruiz de Alcarcón, Hernando. "Tratado de las supersticiones y costumbres gentílicas que oy viven entre los indios naturales desta Nueva España." In *Tratado de las idolatrías, supersticiones, dioses, ritos, hechicerías y otras costumbres gentílicas de las razas aborígenes de México* (edited by Francisco del Paso y Troncoso), vol. 2, pp. 17–180. Mexico: Ediciones Fuente Cultural (Librería Navarro), 1953.

Sahagún, Bernardino de. *Florentine Codex: General History of the Things of New Spain.* Edited by Arthur J. O. Anderson and Charles E. Dibble. Sante Fe: School of American Research and University of Utah, 1950–82.

Sapper, Carl. *Das nördliche Mittel-Amerika nebst einem Ausflug nach dem Hochland von Anahuac: Reisen und Studien aus den Jahren 1888–95.* Brunswick: Friedrich Vieweg & Sohn, 1897.

Schoolcraft, Henry R. *Historical and Statistical Information Respecting the History, Condition and Prospects of the Indian Tribes of the United States.* 6 vols. Philadelphia: Lippincott, 1851–57.

Sodi M., Demetrio. *La literatura de los mayas.* Mexico: Editorial Joaquín Mortiz, 1964.

Spier, Leslie. *Havasupai Ethnography.* Anthropological Papers of the American Museum of Natural History, vol. 29, pt. 3. New York, 1928.

Spinden, Herbert J. *Songs of the Tewa.* New York: Exposition of Indian Tribal Arts, 1933.

Swanton, John R. *Haida Texts and Myths: Skidgate Dialect.* Bureau of American Ethnology Bulletin 29. Washington, 1905.

Thalbitzer, William. "Language and Folklore." Article no. 3 (pp. 113–564) in Part 2 of *The Ammassalik Eskimo: Contributions to the Ethnology of the East Greenland Natives.* Edited by Thalbitzer. This part is vol. 40 of *Meddelelser om Grønland.* Copenhagen: C. A. Reitzel, 1923.

Thompson, J. Eric S. *Ethnology of the Mayas of Southern and Central British Honduras.* Field Museum of Natural History, Anthropological Series, vol. 17, no. 2. Chicago, 1930.

Turner, Lucien M. "Ethnology of the Ungava District, Hudson Bay Territory." *Eleventh Annual Report of the Bureau of American Ethnology, 1889–90,* pp. 159–350. Washington, 1894.

Underhill, Ruth M. *Papago Indian Religion.* New York: Columbia University Press, 1946.

Underhill, Ruth M.; Bahr, D. M.; Lopez, B.; Pancho J.; and Lopez, D. *Rainhouse and Ocean: Speeches for the Papago Year.* Museum of Northern Arizona Press, 1979.

Victor, Paul-Emile. *Poèmes esquimaux.* 2d ed. Paris: Pierre Seghers, [1951].

Voth, H. R. *Oraibi Natal Customs and Ceremonies.* Field Columbian Museum, Anthropological Series, vol. 6, no. 2. Chicago, 1905.

Weltfish, Gene. "Music of the Pawnee." Booklet accompanying Folkways album FE 4334. New York: Folkways Records, 1965.

Wyman, Leland C. *Blessingway.* Tucson: University of Arizona Press, 1970.

GLOSSARY OF TRIBES, CULTURES, AND LANGUAGES

Ammassalik / An Eskimo people of East Greenland.

Anambé / A tribe of the southeastern Amazon basin, Brazil. Now extinct.

Apache / A native people of Arizona and New Mexico, including the Jicarilla, the Mescalero, and the White Mountain Apache.

Arapaho / A Plains tribe of two divisions: the Southern Arapaho, who have settled in Oklahoma, and the Northern Arapaho, now on reservation lands in central Wyoming.

Arara / A tribe of the Xingu River, north central Brazil.

Arekuna / A tribe of eastern Venezuela. Also called Pemón.

Arikara / A tribe of western North Dakota.

Aztec / An advanced culture of the central Mexican highlands, discovered by Cortés in 1519. (In its narrowest use, the term applies to the Mexica, or Aztec Indians of Mexico City, conquered by Cortés in 1521.)

Blackfeet / A tribe of the northern Plains, now on reservation lands in northwestern Montana.

Cágaba / A tribe of the northeastern coast of Colombia.

Cherokee / A native people of the southeastern United States, now divided between North Carolina and Oklahoma.

Chippewa / The largest native tribe north of Mexico, with more than 40,000 members in the United States (mostly in Michigan, Wisconsin, and Minnesota) and perhaps as many as 120,000 in Canada. Also called Ojibwa.

Copper Eskimo / A native people of the Arctic coast in the northeastern part of the District of Mackenzie, Canada.

Creek / A group of native peoples of Georgia and Alabama, now removed to Oklahoma.

Crow / A northern Plains tribe, now mainly confined to a reservation in southern Montana.

Eskimo / A general name for the natives of the Arctic coasts. All the native peoples of the New World may be termed "Indians" except for the Eskimos (also called Inuit), whose distinctive cultural and physical characteristics put them in a class by themselves.

Flathead / A tribe of western Montana.

Haida (HIGH-dah) / The native people of the Queen Charlotte Islands, off the coast of British Columbia, Canada.

Havasupai / A small tribe of the Grand Canyon, northern Arizona.

Hopi / A Pueblo people of northeastern Arizona.

Huichol (wee-CHOL) / A native people of northwestern Mexico.

Iglulik / An Eskimo group north of Hudson Bay. Includes the Aivilik.

Inca / The pre-conquest culture of Andean and coastal Peru.

Jicarilla (hee-kah-REE-yah) / An Apache people of northeastern New Mexico.

Kekchi / A Mayan people of central Guatemala and southern Belize.

Kiowa / A southern Plains tribe with survivors in Oklahoma.

Kwakiutl (kwah-kyootl, with the "ootl" as in "bootleg") / A native people of British Columbia, Canada.

Lingua geral (ling-gwa zheh-RAHL) / A trade language spoken in the Amazon basin of Brazil.

Maya / A general name for the native peoples of Guatemala, also occupying parts of southern Mexico, Belize, and Honduras. Includes the Tzotzil and the Kekchi. (In its narrowest use, the term applies to the Yucatec, or Mayan Indians of the Yucatan Peninsula of Mexico.)

Mazatec / The native people of the town of Huautla de Jiménez and surrounding countryside, south central Mexico.

Mbyá / A native people of Paraguay.

Mescalero / An Apache people of southeastern New Mexico.

Modoc / A native people of northeastern California and southern Oregon.

Navajo / The largest Indian tribe in the United States today, numbering over 100,000 persons, mostly in northeastern Arizona and adjacent New Mexico. The spelling "Navaho," preferred by anthropologists during the period 1900–70, is now falling into disuse.

Netsilik / An Eskimo group northwest of Hudson Bay.

Nootka / A native people occupying the western shore of Vancouver Island, Canada.

Omaha / A tribe of eastern Nebraska.

Papago / A native people of southern Arizona.

Paviotso / A native people of northern Nevada and southeastern Oregon. Also called Northern Paiute.

Pawnee / A once-powerful tribe of the Platte River, now greatly reduced. Survivors are in Oklahoma.

Pueblo / A general name for town-dwelling Indians of New Mexico and Arizona. Includes the Hopi, the Tewa, the Zuni, and several other groups, speaking a variety of languages.

Quechua (KETCH-wuh) / An Andean people (and language) of Ecuador, Peru, and parts of Bolivia, Chile, and Argentina. The language was formerly that of the Incas. Spoken today by approximately five million people.

Seneca / A tribe of western New York and adjacent Canada. One of the six nations of the Iroquois.

Sioux / General name for a group of related tribes of the northern Mississippi Valley, now living on extensive reservations mostly in the Dakotas.

Tewa (TAY-wuh) / A Pueblo people of northern New Mexico, inhabiting six towns, or villages, the largest of which is San Juan.

Tlingit / The native people of the Alaskan panhandle.

Tsimshian / A native people of the northern coast of British Columbia, Canada.

Tzotzil / A Mayan people of the state of Chiapas, southern Mexico.

Uitoto (wee-TOH-toh) / A forest-dwelling people of southeastern Colombia.

White Mountain Apache / An Apache people of eastern Arizona.

Winnebago / A Sioux-related Wisconsin tribe now divided between Wisconsin and Nebraska.

Wintu / A small tribe of the northern California coast.